T0187519

Organization in
Open Source Communities

RIOT! Routledge Studies in Innovation, Organization and Technology

Organization in Open Source Communities

At the Crossroads of the Gift and Market Economies

Evangelia Berdou

Routledge
Taylor & Francis Group

NEW YORK AND LONDON

First published 2011
by Routledge
711 Third Avenue, New York, NY 10017, USA

Simultaneously published in the UK
by Routledge
2 Park Square, Milton Park, Abingdon, Oxon OX14 4RN

Routledge is an imprint of the Taylor & Francis Group, an informa business

© 2011 Taylor & Francis

The right of Evangelia Berdou to be identified as author of this work has been asserted by her in accordance with sections 77 and 78 of the Copyright, Designs and Patents Act 1988.

Typeset in Sabon by IBT Global.

Library of Congress Cataloging-in-Publication Data
Berdou, Evangelia.
Organization in open source communities : at the crossroads of the gift and market economy / by Evangelia Berdou.
 p. cm. — (Routledge studies in innovation, organization and technology ; 15)
 Includes bibliographical references and index.
 1. Open source software--Economic aspects. 2. Open source software—Social aspects. I. Title.
 HF5548.38.O64B47 2010
 338.6—dc22

ISBN13: 978-0-415-48042-0 (hbk)
ISBN13: 978-0-203-85197-5 (ebk)

Contents

Figures

Tables

Acronyms

CoP	Communities of practice
CVS	Concurrent Version System
FAQ	Frequently Asked Questions
FL/OSS	Free/Libre Open Source Software
FSF	Free Software Foundation
GNOME	GNU Network Object Model Environment
GNU	Gnu is not Unix
GPL	General Public License
GUADEC	GNOME Users and Developers European Conference
GUI	Graphical User Interface
HP	Hewlett-Packard
ICTs	Information and communication technologies
IRC	Internet Relay Chat
ISV	Independent Software Vendor
KDE	K Desktop Environment
LGPL	Lesser General Public Licence
MIT	Massachusetts Institute of Technology
MySQL	My Structured Query Language
OSI	Open Source Initiative

PIM   Personal Information Management

QA   Quality Assurance

VCS   Version Control System

Foreword

Some of the most difficult to resolve issues in the Internet era involve questions about the sustainability and transformation of human organizations—what will persist and what will emerge as people make more intensive use of Internet-related technologies? If previous, albeit hierarchical, structures of governance are withering in the face of superior forms of distributed authority that underpin the Internet and the innumerable applications that it supports, what are consequences? These questions are being asked by scholars across the disciplinary spectrum. There are many claims and counterclaims—some supported by empirical evidence, and some not. Some claim that our twenty-first-century configuration of networking technologies represents a gift that generates opportunities for new forms of creative expression, for inclusive democratic participation and for innovative entrepreneurial enterprise. But is it so straightforward?

Are the Internet and the open source software movement the harbingers of a new work ethic, a new mode—or ideology—of sharing and reciprocity which stands in antithesis to the commercial market regime? Analysts and pundits alike seem to gravitate towards extreme positions. Some say we need only promote the ethos of commons-based peer production to ensure a more equitable and open society. Others see these developments as side effects or epiphenomena that are symbiotic with the commercial market, much as popular music groups and authors have built success on anti-commercial or anti-establishment messages. The sceptics ask, who will pay the electricity and rent for these activities and their participants?

In this book, Evangelia Berdou takes up the challenge of providing a measured and empirically grounded account of Free/Libre Open Source Software developers' practices. Developers provide their expertise on both voluntary and paid bases. They develop a growing share of the software upon which we increasingly rely. Berdou's study provides clear evidence that the portrayal of the gift and the market economies as oppositional is misleading. She shows that there is substantial interpenetration of these forms of organization, indicating a hybridization that has yet to stabilize, suggesting that we are well into processes of change that will continue to evolve.

This book provides insights into the complexity of these processes of change. By locating her analysis within both sociology and economics, she highlights key leverage points such as differences in the pace, intensity and coherence of paid versus voluntary contributors. Her analysis suggests immediate applications in the governance of such communities and important starting points for future research.

In the early 1980s when the open distribution of source code (which had been a feature of varying importance over the entire history of the computer industry) became associated with a more specific free software *movement*, few would have imagined that setting free the source code of the operating system software that drives computers would spawn developments that have become issues for policy makers and firms all over the world. In particular, the proliferation of licence types has created gradations in intellectual property protection at a time when this protection is being extended and reinforced. The choice of licensing terms as well as other features has created a major experiment for testing the conditions needed to attract voluntary contributions and observing the choices of firms to share resources in an 'open' domain. All of these developments have turned attention to the governance of the communities producing such software.

Governance involves not only large issues such as the choice of licence for software produced by a community, but also the difficult and sometimes divisive issues regarding technology design choices. Berdou enriches the discussion of communities of practice by considering how power relationships emerge from the pronouncements of community values and purposes in a more explicit way, drawing upon Foucault's insights in a highly practical manner. She considers the complete community—composed not only of 'star' programmers but also of those who expand the reach of open source software by engaging in documentation and language translation activities.

Berdou gives us a particularly insightful treatment of how values, tools and processes converge, establishing open source communities as subjects of governance. The term 'technologies of communities' is used to capture the convergence of authoritative ideals and values, social ties, and tools and techniques for managing and coordinating the software development process. These observations, like others in this book, highlight many opportunities for further research.

Perhaps the most difficult topic which Berdou tackles is the idea of the gift economy. It is clear from recent studies of the motivation of open source contributors that ideologies—that is, normative ideas about how social relations should be conducted—are very significant. The mutual regard and ethical integrity standards that flow from a common belief in the gift economy are extremely useful not only in recruiting participants, but also in bringing people together in discussions of governance systems and processes. The Internet provides unique opportunities for bringing people with shared interests together, even when they are highly dispersed in the offline world. Fostering the principles of a consensual society is an old idea, but one that is shown here to be powerfully re-energized by the open source software movement.

When the gift and market economies intersect, the result is the emergence of a new organizational culture and a new style of economic organization. This book confirms that the mediation of human interactions through software and digital hardware has enormous implications for society and for the sustainability of the economy. This book is a good illustration of why we need to challenge simplistic models of how the new modes of organization are combining with conventional norms and practices.

Professor Robin Mansell
London School of Economics and Political Science

Professor W. Edward Steinmueller
University of Sussex

August 2009

Acknowledgments

I would not have been able to complete this book without financial support from the UK Economic and Social Research Council (ESRC). Their award (PTA-026–27–1479) allowed me the luxury of a year to think broadly about the new models of production that are supported by information and communication technologies. Working with Professor W. Edward Steinmueller gave me the confidence to explore relevant ideas in economics, and during all the stages of writing this book his patient guidance has been invaluable. I benefited enormously from his insights and support. The encouragement and energy of my former PhD supervisor, Professor Robin Mansell, sustained me through those times when I doubted that I could complete this project.

I am also indebted to the FL/OSS contributors who gave of their time so generously during my PhD research, and I am grateful to my colleagues at the Institute of Development Studies for their support and understanding during the last stages of writing. I am thankful to Cynthia Little for her enormous help with the manuscript.

My husband, Alexandros, remains my solid point of reference. His love and support, and that of the rest of my family, have helped me retain perspective during some difficult periods.

1 Introduction

In 2006, Nicholas Carr, a prolific blogger and a successful writer on technology and business, and Yochai Benkler, a professor of law and author of the influential book *The Wealth of Networks*, made an interesting wager on the long-term sustainability of commons-based peer production. The term 'commons-based peer production' was coined by Benkler to describe a new form of economic production in which the efforts of a large number of individuals distributed across the globe are coordinated to produce complex goods without the need for centralized control, and often without monetary reward. Benkler's position was that by 2011 most of the content produced on social media sites—such as Flickr, a popular photo-sharing site, and YouTube, a video-sharing platform—would still be generated by amateurs working without payment. Carr, on the other hand, was convinced that the main reason why these collectives were operating outside the price system was because a market had yet to emerge that puts a price on their contributions and skills.

Benkler perceives these individuals as operating within the gift economy, where the willingness to contribute to the collective effort stems from a desire to accumulate social capital and is underlined by an understanding of the importance of reciprocity in creating a public good. Carr was sceptical that these online amateur collectives would eventually replace professional institutions as the engines of cultural production and technological innovation. He suggests that history has taught us that the trajectory of amateur collectives emerging around new technologies, such as the ham radio or astronomy communities, is usually one of assimilation within dominant market structures. Benkler, on the other hand, consistently argues that commons-based peer production has the capacity to radically transform markets and organizations.

Carr's and Benkler's ideas encapsulate some important aspects of the debate on the viability of emerging forms of collaboration supported by information and communication technologies (ICTs). This debate concerns essentially the transformative powers of individuals and collectives coalescing around shared aims, ideals and technologies. It also concerns issues of transformation—of how these collectives will evolve and, potentially, how they will change as a result of their incorporation into existing market dynamics. The wager made by Carr and Benkler, however, can be somewhat misleading because it is based on the assumption that the gift and exchange economies are mutually exclusive possibilities (i.e., if volunteers contributors persistently outnumber paid individuals, then the gift economy has prevailed). This wager is also misleading because it casts the relationship between voluntary groups or communities and firms as a contest for dominance of the profit-seeking logic of capitalism versus the gift culture's drive for the accumulation of social capital and the willingness to participate in order to benefit from the collective effort.

Experience and accumulated evidence, however, suggest otherwise. Some forms of peer production are becoming intensively commercialized. Free/Libre Open Source Software (FL/OSS) has been commoditized for many years. FL/OSS business ventures, such as the Linux distributors RedHat Inc. and Canonical Ltd, have developed successful products and services based upon software that is freely available for others to use. FL/OSS volunteers coexist with software developers who are employed by companies to work on these projects. The involvement of companies in the development process can be considered a positive sign for the long-term prospects of a software development community. The FL/OSS model of organization is being successfully adopted and adapted by a plethora of businesses, and FL/OSS communities are being initiated, with varying degrees of success, around existing commercial software products.

My argument in this book is positioned between these two extremes. Between the perception of the gift and exchange economies as a contest between contrasting logics of motivation and software production, on the one hand, and their hybridization and successful synthesis, on the other. The story that unfolds is one of tensions and opportunities that are emerging as individuals, firms and collectives pursue their goals and align their interests. It is a story of power relations, of opportunities lost and gained and of productive and problematic tensions, within and across the boundaries of FL/OSS communities. My focus is on the FL/OSS model of organization and on the encounters of actors that participate in the FL/OSS development process. I consider the FL/OSS model of development to be a template for many types of commons-based peer production, and the encounters of the actors that participate in these processes illustrate the possibilities that may be applied in other areas of peer production.

SETTING THE RECORD STRAIGHT ON FL/OSS

To consider FL/OSS as a template for peer production is not to imply that all peer production domains are the same. There are irreducible differences between blogging, Wikipedia, Flickr and FL/OSS in terms of the skills required to participate, the organization of production, ownership of the tools and outputs of collaboration, and the nature of the outputs of these activities. If other expressions of reciprocity in the digital realm are included, such as peer-to-peer file sharing and those which focus on distribution, then the gift economy landscape becomes even more complex. The diversity of gift economies is present in FL/OSS production, and the experiences, practices and norms that inspire FL/OSS development vary significantly across projects and contexts. For example, the distribution of decision-making authority over the direction of a FL/OSS project among its contributors does not usually apply to FL/OSS projects initiated by firms where control usually remains with the founding firm. In this book I examine the factors that motivate collaboration in two types of FL/OSS projects: those initiated and managed by firms and those initiated and managed by communities. By comparing these two—the first controlled principally by firms and the second governed through distributed authority—I show how the social dynamics of peer production interact with market dynamics. The results of this interaction have many implications for the division of labour and the evolution of FL/OSS communities. Improving the quality of the software user's experience and catering to the needs of specialized users and those users who are underserved by the market increasingly require the mobilization of skills other than programming. I emphasize the range and importance of non-programming contributions for the sustainability of FL/OSS projects.

The diversity that emerges from the way that different FL/OSS principles, processes and tools are interpreted and realized across various contexts has led to a great deal of misunderstanding about what the FL/OSS model of development involves and what types of software can be subsumed within it. To address some of these misconceptions and to set the scene for the view of FL/OSS communities that emerges in this book, a few basic facts about FL/OSS and the FL/OSS model of development are important to keep in mind.

The term FL/OSS describes software protected under special copyright licences aimed at ensuring availability and free (re)distribution of the source code.[1] It refers also to a paradigm of decentralized collaboration and production that incorporates some unique technical and social characteristics. FL/OSS is frequently identified with a movement founded on the ideals of the hacker culture and espousing the idea of community. It is increasingly being associated with the new business models, inspired by approaches that emphasize the innovative potential of expert users[2] that are emerging as firms attempt to learn how to profit from innovations developed outside their boundaries—in collaboration with clients and expert user communities.

FL/OSS licences are an important institutional innovation. They were developed in order to prevent the appropriation of software code in a manner that would restrict free access by other users. Essentially, FL/OSS licences use copyright in order to enable rather than to restrict user freedom.

FL/OSS licences use copyright law to constrain those who might want to restrict the rights of others. This innovation has inspired the creation of licences, such as those generated by the Creative Commons movement, that enable individuals to share, remix and reuse various kinds of information. Generally speaking, there are two main types of FL/OSS licences: copyleft and non-copyleft (Lessig, 2002). The best-known example of a copyleft licence is the GNU[3] General Public License (GPL). The requirement of a GPL is that any software derived from GPLed software is placed under the same terms as the GPL and this is regarded as a disincentive to commercial exploitation. For example, firms wanting to combine FL/OSS with pro- prietary code are required to license the resulting software under a GPL. Non-copyleft licences address business requirements and provide for more flexibility in mixing proprietary and FL/OSS by imposing fewer restrictions on the use and distribution of the resulting software (Lessig, 2002).

Differences in licensing terms reflect important differences in priorities within the FL/OSS movement. The GPL exemplifies the stance taken by Richard Stallman and the Free Software Foundation (FSF), which priori- tizes the ethical and philosophical commitment of the movement and, spe- cifically, the notion of 'freedom' over commercial exploitation. The desire for an approach to FL/OSS that would be less restrictive for business led to the creation in 1998 of the Open Source Initiative (OSI). FL/OSS develop- ers who adhere to the principles of this organization tend to emphasize the technical superiority of FL/OSS in comparison to proprietary alternatives and the efficiency of the collaborative model of FL/OSS development as compared to traditional software development approaches.

Prominent examples of FL/OSS software include the GNU/Linux operat- ing system, the Apache server program and the Python computer language. Initially, most of the software produced by the FL/OSS movement was in support of computer operating systems. This meant that early users consisted mostly of programmers and system administrators, and very few applica- tions were addressed to the average, non-technical user. However, this is rap- idly changing. FL/OSS is being adopted by a growing number of public and private organizations and is reaching a wider and more diverse non-technical user base. A report released in 2006 (Ghosh, 2006) on the economic impact of FL/OSS in the European ICT sector indicates that the market share of FL/OSS is substantial, with many public and private organizations reporting their use of FL/OSS programs in numerous applications domains.

The recent popularity of FL/OSS belies the movement's long history and connections to older institutions. The tradition of sharing and cooperation that underlies the FL/OSS model of software production can be traced to the early days of software development in the 1950s. It is founded on an engineering culture that emerged from the major US academic institutions such as Massachussetts Institute of Technology (MIT), the University of California at Berkeley and the Carnegie Mellon Institute. This tradition is associated with a set of values that forms the basis of what is widely known as the 'hacker culture', whose prominent features are the freedom to access and share information, the pursuit of technical excellence and the joy of creativity (Castells, 2001; Himanen, 2001; Levy, 1984). The emphasis on transparency, the free flow of information and the significance attributed to peer review as a necessary aspect of the processes of bettering one's skills and collective knowledge has led some to draw parallels between FL/OSS and science—and particularly the 'republic of science' (Polanyi, 1962). Compared to proprietary science, which is dominated by market interests, the republic of science is said to be driven by the pursuit of knowledge and is founded on practices promoting the open communication of research findings (Dasgupta and David, 1994).

A decline in the freedom valued by hackers resulting from commercial software companies withholding the sources of software programs, motivated Richard Stallman to build his FSF in 1985. One of the initial goals of the FSF was to create a functioning clone of Unix, the operating system that was developed in the 1960s and 1970s by a group of employees at AT&T (American Telephone and Telegraph Co.) and that was commercialized in the 1980s. The development that marked the take-off of the FL/OSS movement was introduced by a Finnish computing science student, Linus Torvalds. Torvalds created the kernel of the Linux operating system, a program that has been regarded as the leading, potential challenger to Microsoft Windows. Linux's model of decentralized development, which involves hundreds of globally distributed contributors, appears to question the validity of the received doctrines of software development and management, such as 'Brooks's law' (1995). This law states that the more complex a project becomes, the more problematic is the communication within the team of programmers, leading to a downward spiralling of productivity. Many researchers and practitioners have tried to discover what makes the FL/OSS development model so successful. Several arguments are often invoked in discussions about the efficiency of the FL/OSS development approach in comparison to traditional software development models.

A characteristic of FL/OSS development that is seen to mitigate the important communication costs of traditional software development is modularity. Modularity 'describes the extent to which [software] can be broken down into smaller components, or modules, that can be independently produced before they are assembled into a whole' (Benkler, 2006: 100). In the software production context described by Brooks, the tightly integrated character of the systems under development necessitated management from the top and intensive communication among developers because even minor changes would have knock-on effects on the operation of a system. In modular systems, however, complexity is reduced by the existence of clear, visible rules about how the different components of the system work together. This enables programmers to work on the parts of the software they are interested in without having to have in-depth knowledge about how other parts of the code base work. Nevertheless, as I show later, modularity is not a 'silver bullet', and there are numerous barriers to entry for new software developers.

FL/OSS development, similar to other types of peer production, is about strength in numbers: the cumulative effect of many, small and large contributions. Modularity and FL/OSS development tools, such as a version control system (VCS),[4] enable individuals to pursue different solutions in parallel, making it possible for their contributions to be drawn together easily. The process of peer review is said to support the selection of the best solutions from among the many and to help contributors to hone their programming skills. The replication of effort associated with parallel development is regarded as evidence of an abundance of labour that is consistent with the principles of the gift economy. The ability afforded by FL/OSS tools to revert easily to more stable versions of a program when experimental ones do not function properly is seen as encouraging experimentation and innovation. Another factor that sustains the interest of volunteers and the momentum of development is the practice of frequent releases of new versions of the software. Nonetheless, as I demonstrate in the chapters in this book, not all FL/OSS manages to attract large numbers of contributors or achieves a stage in its development when the smallest, incremental contributions can lead to substantial progress.

I propose a different perspective for understanding the dynamics underlying cooperation in FL/OSS communities than the lens of project attributes. My perspective considers how projects are managed and funded and the social and technical characteristics of the FL/OSS production process presented. This view involves three principles for organizing and sustaining participation in FL/OSS communities which are grouped together as 'technologies of communities'. The first principle concerns the basis of emergent, distributed authority within FL/OSS projects and its resulting social organization which, I show, is associated with the idea of meritocracy. The second principle concerns the significance of the invocation of community to (re)affirm a common basis for participation and enable the different actors to position themselves strategically in the FL/OSS production space. The third principle involves the tools and techniques for managing FL/OSS communities. I show that many of the tools and techniques used in FL/OSS production are instrumental in rendering concrete the space of social production, allowing FL/OSS communities to govern themselves or enabling others to govern them. When combined with an understanding of the multiple connections that develop between businesses and social communities, the view of FL/OSS that emerges through the lens of these principles leads to interesting conclusions about the evolution and the transformative potential of FL/OSS and the FL/OSS model of organization.

THE PROMISE OF FL/OSS AND PEER PRODUCTION

Before embarking on the main part of the FL/OSS story, it is necessary to clarify why peer production, and FL/OSS in particular, have attracted so much attention and fostered so many expectations, and what, in my view, is really at stake. FL/OSS captures the imagination of those who discover how unconventional the process through which software, such as the GNU/Linux operating system and Firefox, the popular web browser, is produced compared to conventional software development. Part of FL/OSS's appeal lies in its subversiveness, its capacity to throw open to question established ideas about what drives economic production and what makes production efficient. In some respects the success of FL/OSS vindicates countercultural ideals regarding what can be achieved when motivated individuals coalesce around technologies to form communities driven by shared values and ideas. Another major reason for the popularity of FL/OSS lies in its ability to illustrate the emerging possibilities for collaboration supported by ICTs. In this context even the smallest, seemingly most inconsequential contributions can accumulate and contribute towards the creation of software goods that traditional organizations would find difficult to replicate. FL/OSS's true power seems to rest on in its ability to synthesize the most diverse contributions made by individuals motivated by equally diverse priorities, such as the value derived from the use of the software, the fascination with and satisfaction from programming and, in some cases, the monetary rewards to be obtained from involvement.

In this book I examine the elision between the ideas of sociality, community, efficiency and economic production in order to assess the challenges and the opportunities that emerge from an overlay of social and market relations. I argue that the promise of FL/OSS lies in how it reconfigures the relationship between the gift and market economies, that is, the relationship between sociality and economic production. The idea that these two spheres of economic activity can coexist and co-develop is not new. Although the gift economy refers to socially embedded forms of economic relations associated with pre-capitalist societies, it is also bound up with the activities within capitalist societies, such as some aspects of science, religion, charity and community groups, that are organized explicitly to avoid key elements of market organization. In contrast to the market economy, where commodity and monetary exchanges are driven by the pursuit of pecuniary gain and take place within a space shaped by scarcity and impersonal efficiency, the gift economy is seen to constitute a system of transactions among individuals in support of mutual empowerment and collective production. The importance of these transactions, although recognized in some areas of the social sciences, such as the field of economic sociology, has been largely ignored by most mainstream neoclassical economists.

The promise of FL/OSS and peer production lies in the fact that it appears to reverse the terms of this relationship between sociality and economic production by empowering individuals and collectives to challenge existing market institutions. However, the implications of reconfiguring the relationship between the gift and the market economies are far from transparent and, indeed, are often surprising.

My analysis in this book highlights several aspects of this relationship. In Chapter 2, I present a toolbox of ideas that is drawn upon throughout the book to discuss the transformation and transformative potential of FL/OSS. This includes three ideas, first the idea of 'technologies of communities' that I introduced earlier, and second, the idea of large FL/OSS communities as 'constellations of communities of practice', that is, of groups of contributors that are characterized by different priorities and skills sets. The third idea is that of embeddedness. Mature FL/OSS projects are shown to be situated (embedded) within existing markets. The idea of FL/OSS communities as 'embedded constellations of practice' allows me to develop an original account of the way that the division of labour in FL/OSS is affected by the increasing adoption of this type of software development. In Chapter 3, I discuss an issue that some would consider secondary to other questions posed by the success of FL/OSS: the methodological aspects of FL/OSS studies. I consider these to be crucial because they are the deciding factors in what aspects of FL/OSS and its diversity we choose to focus on or to ignore.

In Chapter 4, I discuss how firms use FL/OSS to learn and to expand their markets and how they try to maintain a stream of external contributions around their products by cultivating the idea of community. How firms become involved in FL/OSS communities and how their presence, in terms of the importance of the roles of employed FL/OSS contributors, influences these communities are the issues examined in Chapter 5. In Chapter 6 attention is drawn to diversity within the context of FL/OSS communities and to the complex division of labour that underpins mature FL/OSS projects. In Chapter 7, I consider how the role of firms in FL/OSS and an understanding of the FL/OSS model of organization can reveal a better understanding of the transformation and transformative potential of FL/OSS. In the final chapter of this volume, Chapter 8, I discuss the implications of a reconfigured relationship between sociality and economic production.

2 Technologies of Communities and Peer Production
Disentangling Power Relations in FL/OSS Development

The FL/OSS model of organization appears to be continuously adopted, adapted and extended in new contexts and domains of intellectual work. Modularity, peer review, transparency and the intensive use of an array of specialized and more widely distributed online tools are used to organize the contributions of hundreds and sometimes thousands of contributors. Wikipedia has applied the same principles of decentralization, peer review and open access to organize and mobilize volunteers to create the world's largest and most contributed to encyclopaedia. Firms are releasing software under FL/OSS licences and adopting FL/OSS development tools to encourage innovation around their products, both within and across firm boundaries. 'Crowdsourcing', a novel problem-solving and production model, adopts the FL/OSS principle of decentralization for the completion of small, very precisely defined tasks that often do not require specialized skills (Brabham, 2008).

How can fad be distinguished from legitimate change? How can we identify trends from emerging regularities that may hint at more lasting impacts? Some explanations, such as Eric Raymond's (2001) metaphor of FL/OSS development as a bustling, self-organizing bazaar that carries echoes of a libertarian utopia, are seen to encapsulate the idea of FL/OSS. These explanations and metaphors, however, are part of the story of the evolution of the FL/OSS phenomenon. They are indicative of how people perceive FL/OSS and the FL/OSS model of organization in revealing the aspirations or misconceptions that have become invested in the ideas of community, collaboration and bottom-up forms of organization supported by ICTs. More systematic approaches relate the FL/OSS phenomenon to processes and institutions, by drawing on established bodies of social theory. In Chapter 1, I argued that the FL/OSS model describes the continuous transformation of the gift economy and can be seen also as an adaptation and extension of older social institutions such as the republic of science.[1] Others have approached the FL/OSS model of development as a potentially new type of governance structure, a coordination mechanism that is distinctive from those employed to motivate and organize economic production in the context of markets and firms (Benkler, 2002; Demil and

Lecocq, 2006).[2] Yet other lines of enquiry emphasize how FL/OSS and the FL/OSS model are being transformed and appropriated within existing business strategies and market flows (Fitzgerald, 2006; Fosfuri et al., 2008; West, 2003). In the literature and in the emergent popular understanding of FL/OSS, accounts that argue in favour of its distinctiveness alternate with accounts that emphasize its transformative nature or character. The depth and richness of these explanations, social science based or otherwise, depend on how successfully they situate the FL/OSS phenomenon within the dynamics of institutional change and innovation, on the one hand, and the forces of continuity and appropriation, on the other.

In this chapter I draw on three theoretical traditions to build a set of concepts that can be used to examine the FL/OSS model of organization as a new way of configuring relations of power among groups, individuals and firms. This includes concepts drawn from the communities of practice (CoP) perspective and some strands of economic sociology concerned with the notion of embeddedness, as well as Foucault's work on the nature and function of power. Each perspective highlights a different, previously under-examined aspect of the FL/OSS model of organization. Together, these three theoretical traditions create a framework for an examination that allows us to disentangle the dependencies that form between the gift and market economies as firms, communities and individuals negotiate their priorities and interests.

COMMUNITIES AS EMERGING SPACES OF PRODUCTION AND INNOVATION

Interest in the role of community in knowledge production and innovation is increasing (Amin and Roberts, 2008; Dahlander et al., 2008). Such notions as epistemic cultures, epistemic communities and CoP have been formulated to express the importance being attributed to communities as repositories of knowledge and havens of innovation. ICTs have been instrumental through their role in enabling traditional knowledge communities to evolve into distributed communities, transcending the confines of space and time, and supporting the formation and, indeed, the design of new communities.

These various notions, which in one way or another stress the links between community, work and creativity, have emerged in different contexts. Peter Haas (1992) formulated the notion of epistemic communities within the framework of international policy coordination and international relations. Epistemic communities are networks of professionals with recognized expertise who share normative and causal beliefs, notions of validity and policy goals. Knorr-Cetina (1999: 1) studied the role of epistemic cultures which she defined as 'those amalgams of arrangements and mechanisms bonded-through affinity and historical coincidence-which in a given field, make up how we know what we know'. Research on the dynamics of innovation has highlighted the role of technical communities and communities of lead users in interpreting and improving upon technological designs introduced by firms (Rosenkopf and Tushman, 1994; von Hippel, 2007). And Lave and Wenger (1991) developed the idea of a CoP as a theory of learning and socialization in such disparate groups as Mayan midwives in Yucatec, a recovering alcoholics group, meat cutters in a supermarket, US navy quartermasters and Vai and Golan tailors in Liberia.

Despite their different points of origin, these ideas about how expert and occupational groups function share some important characteristics. For example, all of them regard learning and information exchange as inherently social processes. Within such communities the development and recognition of expertise involves a process of socialization into the norms, values and practices of a network of individuals who are involved in similar pursuits and who share an interest in mutual aid and interaction (Steinmueller, 2003). Broadly speaking, these communities operate as spaces that facilitate knowledge sharing through the creation of common vocabularies and storytelling and learning through practice, and the engagement of their members in work and problem solving. These communities, which may be localized or distributed in character, transcend formal organizational boundaries and managerial hierarchies and enable the rapid propagation of information among community members through the bonds of trust that are created.[3]

The potential of occupational and expert communities for fostering creativity and innovation has given rise to a significant body of work that is concerned with their cultivation and deployment by organizations (Swan et al., 2002; Wenger et al., 2002). As indicated by the large number of FL/OSS projects that fail to take off, positive results are far from guaranteed, and invocation on its own of the idea of community—by individuals or firms—is not enough to mobilize commitment and participation. In Chapter 3, I examine how these issues are expressed in FL/OSS projects founded and managed by firms, and highlight some the factors that affect volunteers' decisions to participate in such communities. The idea of a community built around common interests and the value provided by the support of companies keen to attract volunteers are not always enough to secure their participation.

FL/OSS COMMUNITIES AS CONSTELLATIONS OF PRACTICE

The CoP approach offers an intuitive means of understanding the organization of FL/OSS projects. Lave and Wenger (1991) define CoP as being based on triadic relations between 'masters' (old timers), 'young masters' (or journeymen) and 'apprentices' (or newcomers), which renders their dynamics very different from those in a teacher-student relationship. As apprentices, newcomers essentially must learn from the masters, but their learning must also involve some contribution to the community, usually the execution of routine tasks. As the skills of the newcomers evolve and they adopt the community's ways, they are enabled to move gradually from the periphery, where, assuming they have been accepted, they hold the status of legitimate peripheral members, to the centre which is populated by the most experienced and skilled members.

Similar divisions have been observed in other empirically grounded FL/OSS studies. Numerous studies on FL/OSS developers' patterns of communication and contribution point to a relatively small group of contributors who are responsible for the bulk of the activity in their project. This core group of developers appears to be surrounded by a larger group of less-engaged or less-skilled contributors. The core-periphery division has provided the basis for the development of a more elaborate model of the social structure of FL/OSS projects that has come to be known as the onion model of FL/OSS organization (Crowston and Howison, 2005; David and Rullani, 2008). In this model, the core group of skilled developers consists of people with the greatest authority and decision-making power with regard to how the project evolves. This group includes the project founders; the maintainers, that is, the developers in charge of the smooth operation of certain parts of the code base; the most engaged contributors; and the developers, who assume critical coordinating roles, such as that of managing the release process for each new version of the program. The next layer of the onion includes those programmers who contribute relatively small changes or patches to the code base. Their contributions are usually subject to review by the maintainers before acceptance. The next layer is populated by involved users, who provide feedback on how the program works by reporting faults ('bugs' in the language of software development) and by suggesting improvements either by participating in the project forums or by employing more specialized tools, such as bug databases. The outermost layer of the onion includes the constituency of the program's users and individuals (often described as lurkers) who observe the community's online discussions and have an interest in development, but who do not contribute. This division of roles and the corresponding decision-making power is consistent with practitioner accounts regarding the emergent, social basis of participation. In this context an individual's status in the community is not dictated by bureaucracy, but is a result of a proven (or unproven) level of skill, commitment and peer recognition. FL/OSS contributors often adopt a language that invokes the idea of a form of community that is organized around the practice and perfection of the craft of programming. In the peer certification system of the Advogato community, for example, FL/OSS contributors certify each other at the level of journeyman, apprentice or master.

The idea of the socialization of new contributors as a process of enculturation into the values, norms and practices of the hacker culture, and the importance ascribed to the ideological aspects of participation, have dominated popular understanding about the reasons behind the success of the FL/OSS movement. In particular, emphasis on the communal cultural aspects of practice, on the one hand, and interest in the use of FL/OSS communities to support organizational effectiveness and performance, on the other, have overshadowed the equally important, but less harmonizing, aspects of community life that are associated with issues of power and access. As we will see, the study of these issues sheds a different light on the meaning of participation and the organization of FL/OSS communities.

As in traditional CoP, in FL/OSS communities, access is a direct expression of power. Lave and Wenger (1991) examine this aspect through the example of apprentice meat cutters. In this case, newcomers were granted the status of apprentice, but were denied access to the more mature community practices. Thus, newcomers were granted peripherality, but were denied legitimacy. Wenger (1998) addresses the issue of participation by pointing to the difference between peripherality and marginality. Peripherality is conceived as an experience of non-participation that acts as an incentive for the pursuit of deeper involvement, whereas marginality is defined as a negative experience of non-participation that results in a sense of exclusion. Relations of inequality and hierarchy, therefore, are established primarily within a CoP through the granting or denial of status to would-be members.

A closer look at mature, FL/OSS communities that are initiated and managed independently of firms, such as Apache, GNOME or KDE, reveals the complexity of controlling access in an online distributed environment where, in principle, everyone is allowed to participate and where skill and commitment are difficult to judge initially. In the course of my analysis in this book I direct attention to the range of FL/OSS related practices and processes that establish a more complex and graduated idea of membership than the one implied by Lave and Wenger or by the onion model of participation. The availability of source code and ease of signing up as a contributor do not ensure access to more important levels of information or decision making, such as the ability to inform the direction of the project. Although obtaining the right to incorporate changes in the code base is considered by many to be a de facto sign of membership, there are other levels of access, such as becoming a member of a project's administrative body or a member of the technical committee that steers development. In addition, in some projects, having an email address with the project's domain name is a more evident sign of membership—especially to the outside world—than being allowed to commit to the software development tree. Controlling access to an email account confers control over who is seen as being a member of the project and who effectively has the right to represent the community. The fluid boundaries of many FL/OSS communities, combined with the principle of open participation, appear to allow for a more flexible definition of membership than that characterizing more traditional apprenticeship contexts. However, participation in large FL/OSS communities, especially those founded and governed independently of firms, is carefully (re)structured through the formal and informal regulation of different levels of access in decision-making processes, people and resources. As a result, new structures emerge that are a blend of the emergent and of the designed. In commercially initiated and controlled FL/OSS, where control over the acceptance of contributions and the direction of the project is retained largely by firms, access to the core is usually restricted to the initiator firm's employees. In order to invite and sustain external contributions, however, firms cannot be seen to dominate the process of development. In Chapter 3, I consider in detail the balance between control and access in corporately initiated and controlled FL/OSS projects.

Additional constraints regulating the movement between the project's core and periphery are introduced by the online social network characteristics of FL/OSS communities. The core-periphery structure that has been observed in many FL/OSS communities is regarded as being typical of emergent, scale-free networks, which consist of a relatively small number of nodes, in this case FL/OSS contributors, forming the project's core, who are highly connected in terms of ties established through mutual cooperation and communication, and a larger periphery consisting of nodes that are loosely connected through ties based on communication or collaboration with one another. Networks of this type grow through preferential attachment, which means that the more connected a node, the more likely there will be links consolidated with other nodes. This introduces important constrains on the position an individual is likely to attain, because, according to this statistical property, a network's growth is likely to reify the positions of central individuals.

Examination of the internal dynamics of collaboration is crucial for understanding the unique characteristics of the FL/OSS model of organization. Volunteer FL/OSS communities do not exist in a void, but are part of the existing market dynamics. Many FL/OSS projects provide alternatives to proprietary solutions, address emerging market needs and are used to drive demand for complementary goods and services. In Chapter 4, I consider the different business strategies that have developed around FL/OSS.

EMBEDDEDNESS OF FL/OSS COMMUNITIES IN MARKET DYNAMICS

FL/OSS contributors also constitute part of the social networks that become more clearly connected to established professional networks as FL/OSS projects consolidate their links with the market economy. One study on the development of the Linux kernel reveals that between 2005 and 2008, firm-employed developers were responsible for 70% of the work (Kroah-Hartman et al., 2008). The interpenetration of business and social relations is expressed in the idea of embeddedness developed by the American sociologist Mark Granovetter.[4] Granovetter (1985: 483) developed this idea in part to respond to what he regards as 'undersocialized' and 'oversocialized' accounts of human action. Undersocialized accounts are consistent with the perspective of neoclassical economics as 'disallow[ing] by hypothesis any impact of social structure and social relations on production, distribution and consumption'. Oversocialized accounts, which are common in some branches of sociology, including the dominant interpretation of the CoP perspective, emphasize the importance of social processes, norms and values, at the expense of the political and economic structures permeating many aspects of economic life. In this book I extend Granovetter's definition of embeddedness to examine how economic relations are reaffirmed in the social space of community-driven FL/OSS through the importance of employment relations. In Chapter 5, I analyse this aspect of FL/OSS by considering the role of employed developers in the GNOME and KDE projects, two established FL/OSS projects that are introduced and managed independently of firms. In Chapter 6, I consider how the pressures of commercialization and the demands of production amplify the role of learning as a control mechanism that regulates access to the cores of these projects.

The prominence of employed contributors in commercialized FL/OSS communities raises the question of whether they constitute a community of practice distinct from that of volunteers. A more careful look at the nature of tasks performed in large FL/OSS communities introduces another layer of complexity and invites us to rethink the idea of peripheral participation as the first step in a progression towards the centre. The CoP approach assumes that all peripheral members are newcomers who are eager to make their way to the next level of initiation. The research that forms the core of this book, however, indicates that in many cases, primary communities of programmers are complemented by groups of individuals who work on non-programming tasks, such as translation, documentation, creating artwork and managing community public relations. Some of these individuals may be peripheral contributors in Lave and Wenger's (1991) sense, that is, programmers who make the decision to contribute to a less demanding part of a project as a learning strategy that will allow them to move on to programming. However, many supporting or peripheral tasks are carried out by people with no desire to move to the centre of the developer community. In order to examine these aspects of peripherality I adopt the view of FL/OSS projects as constellations of practices (Wenger, 1998), that is, as configurations of diverse, but interconnected, CoP. Wenger develops this idea to describe the variety of CoP that gives life to organizations. My discussion of the characteristics and organization of teams of translators and documenters in Chapter 6 highlights forms of contribution and peripheral participation that are not often examined. The concept of a constellation of practice and my interpretation of the idea of embeddedness, however, are not adequate for examining the deeper, transformative potential of FL/OSS.

To approach this issue I employ the idea of power and the approach to its study suggested by the French philosopher Michel Foucault.

TECHNOLOGIES OF COMMUNITIES AND RELATIONS OF POWER

If the onion model has emerged as the prevailing model for conceptualizing the different roles people assume within FL/OSS communities, then the principal framework for understanding the factors that influence how interactions are organized within the space of FL/OSS projects is that of an 'architecture of participation'. This term was introduced by Tim O'Reilly (2005: 474), who used it to describe 'the nature of systems that are designed for user contribution'. O'Reilly's initial interpretation of this idea refers primarily to the modular nature of FL/OSS projects—the fact that they can be broken down into separate, relatively self-contained parts which, together, form a program or application. The notion of the architecture of participation has been extended to describe the possibilities for participation and cooperation that arise through different choices made at the level of technical design, legal framework and governance (West and O'Mahony, 2008). Such choices include those over who has the power to decide on the direction of a project (distributed authority versus technical committee or company), how easily the software that is being produced can be used as part of a commercial solution (permissive versus restrictive FL/OSS licences) and issues of ownership of copyright (whether by an individual or transferred to third party, such as a project foundation or a company).

Foucault argues that architecture is an important expression of power. In his book *Discipline and Punish* (1979) he uses the Panopticon, an architectural innovation of Jeremy Bentham, as the sign and model of a particular type of societal organization: the disciplinary society. The Panopticon was designed to introduce and establish hierarchical observation and provide the means for the integration of utility, production and control that is characteristic of capitalist production. Adopted not only in prisons but also in factories, schools and hospitals, this model, Foucault argues, integrates into the architecture and geometry of these institutions the distinctive arrangements of observation and close surveillance. His discussion of the dynamics that unfold around the design of the Panopticon and the historical origins of many of the practices that complement its functioning are characteristic of his ideas on the relational, productive and historical character of power (Foucault, 1979).

Power, according to the relational view, is neither a zero-sum game, in which different actors compete for resources and someone's gain is another's loss, nor is it something that is given or exchanged; rather, it is something that is exercised. It is a force that creates complex dependencies and invites a diversity of initiations and reactions on the part of the people involved and whose results are at once productive and ambiguous. The Panopticon helps organize experiments that produce knowledge about the individuals being observed. As Foucault (1979: 204) remarks, it:

> functions as a kind of laboratory for power. Thanks to its mechanisms of observation, it gains in efficiency and in the ability to penetrate into men's behaviour; knowledge follows the advances of power, discovering new objects knowledge over all the surfaces in which power is exercised.

Prison wardens, for example, need to conform to the prisoners' rigorous regimes, and managers may be subjected to the same processes of surveillance and meticulous evaluation as their subordinates. This does not mean that relations of power are symmetrical, but that power always creates complex dependencies among the actors that operate within a given space. A compelling account of the relational character of power is provided by Shoshana Zuboff in her well-known book *In the Age of the Smart Machine* (1988). Zuboff shows how the introduction of information technologies in very different organizational settings improved the automation of production, while rendering the actions of employees more transparent by producing a constant stream of data on their actions. This new visibility affected how relations between senior management, middle management and factory floor workers were negotiated.

My contention is that several aspects of cooperation in FL/OSS are equally ambiguous and relational, hinging on complex interdependencies among various actors. The fact that the majority of contributors to FL/OSS are volunteers and, therefore, in principle can turn their backs on a project if things do not work out as they want, does not erase power relations. It rather establishes a framework of relations, a space of interaction, where the dependencies and their underlying power dynamics are different from those created in the context of traditional organizations, where relations are mediated through formal employment contracts. If we apply this lens to the idea of FL/OSS communities as constellations of practice, then really interesting insights emerge about the nature of these relations and the dynamics upon which they hinge.

Foucault contrasts his relational approach to power to the view of power inscribed in political economy, which, in his opinion, is mistakenly preoccupied with problems of sovereignty and perceives power solely as domination. Although he acknowledges that groups and individuals make conscious and intentional choices that render power relations intelligible, he denies the possibility that the broader consequences of these actions could be coordinated (Foucault, 1982a). As a consequence, Foucault insists that power relations should be examined, not at the level of institutions (the higher level rules and norms that guide the actions of individuals and regulate their relations) because their logic is set and, therefore, difficult to penetrate.

Instead, he suggests that it is better to focus on the lower level practices and techniques that underlie institutions. These he perceives as migrating across time and institutions, occasionally coalescing into specific ways of thinking and action, which, in time, assume the patina of the 'natural' and form the basis for the production of new types of knowledge. Foucault (1981) defines the conceptual terrain in which knowledge is formed and produced as discourse. The idea of discourse in his work takes on the meaning of the dominant rationality that specifies what can be conceived and expressed within a given era and field of activity. Compared to other definitions of discourse which emphasize its textual linguistic dimensions, Foucault's definition of discourse is closely related to the idea of practice. In fact, Foucault conceives of discourse as a form of practice. In his essay 'Questions of Method' (Foucault, 2002: 230) he says that his aim is to examine the relationship between 'a code which rules ways of ruling (how people are to be graded and examined) and a production of true discourses which serve to find, justify and provide reasons and principles for these ways of doing things'.

In the context of FL/OSS, the prevalent discourses evolve around the idea of community which is associated with a more 'natural' way of ordering relations than that imposed in a formal work environment. This explanation provides the principal form of rationalization of power differentials in FL/OSS communities: those who contribute and participate in a certain way have more 'say' than others. The predominance of social organization implicit in the idea of community is often associated, in turn, with ideas of emergence and self-organization in both practitioners' and academics' accounts. This way of thinking tends to underestimate the tensions that arise out of the heterogeneous character of FL/OSS communities—the fact that they are comprised of multiple communities of practice and the importance of their embeddedness in material flows. In my account in this book, I peel back the layers of meaning in the central assumptions related to social organization in FL/OSS by examining the issues of power and authority and by identifying practices, rules and processes that substantiate access and status.

How do Foucault's ideas help us to assess the transformative potential of FL/OSS without underestimating its historical character and its rootedness in existing market dynamics? This is best illustrated by explaining how Foucault perceives the historical evolution of different paradigms of power. Like the economy of production, whose history is the basis of Marxist theory, power, according to Foucault, has its own economy and its own history. In reconstructing the history of the economy of power, he distinguishes between three different configurations of power: (i) sovereign power, in which power emanates from a single, god-given source, the regent; (ii) disciplinary power, which is studied within the context of the formation of institutions such as prisons or hospitals, where the goal of power is to produce docile bodies; and (iii) bio-power, a more recent expression of power, a function of government whose objects are populations and their welfare.

Foucault grounds his analysis of the shift in the predominance of different economies of power in different periods of change in the dominant historical rationality, in the ways that people think and act. His account of the emergence of disciplinary power, which he perceives as the dominant paradigm of power in capitalist society, is not a neat account of the gradual substitution of sovereign power by the new paradigm, but a complex and rich story of the way that different localized requirements helped develop a set of techniques that migrated from one institution to another and imbued existing practices and norms with new meaning. Each new economy of power does not simply erase the power configurations that are implicit in the previous paradigm; they transform its discourse, assimilate many of its procedures and practices and sometimes coexist with it. For example, in *Discipline and Punish* Foucault (1979) describes how the knowledge of organizing and distributing bodies in space and time necessitated by the adoption of the rifle and subsequent changes in military tactics informed industrial organization on the factory floor. This meticulous control of presence and activity, which he calls cellular power, was not entirely new, however; it had been formulated and practised for hundreds of years in monastic communities. It took off, he argues, as the dominant way of organizing as a result of the congruence of a series of complex events, some of which were linked to the rise of the bourgeoisie. It is the connections between practices, knowledge and the effects of generalization of initially localized demands and needs that make Foucault's account of the emergence of different forms of power so compelling. By problematizing the present and the 'natural' function of institutions, Foucault seems to be highlighting the subtle interdependencies between existing and emergent discourses and strategies and creating an alternative account of the way power operates. Although he draws attention principally to the totalizing aspects of power, he argues with vigour that the function of institutions can never be fully realized. This is because of the numerous different, and often competing, strategies deployed within their contexts. Foucault (2002) describes what happens in prisons as a 'witches brew' compared to the beautiful simplicity of the 'Benthamite machine'. This relational, material and historical view of power invites us to examine FL/OSS projects, not as closed systems that lack historical and material connections with the offline world, but as potentially new forms of organization informed by existing practices and discourses that circulate through different domains and institutions.

In this book I use the concept of 'technologies of communities' to explain how different practices, discourses and ideas, some of which are rooted in the hacker culture, others of which are related to the contributors' work experience, converge to create a framework that establishes FL/OSS communities as subjects and objects of governance, that is, capable of determining their own fates, but also vulnerable to exploitation. Foucault elaborates the idea of technology in 'The Political Technology of Individuals' (Foucault, 1982b) and the 'Technologies of the Self' (Foucault, 1982c).

The concept of technology forms part of the vocabulary and the methods that he develops in order to examine the historicity and evolution of different forms of power and the interplay between knowledge and power. In 'Technologies of the Self' Foucault distinguishes between four different types of technology: (i) technologies of production, which allow us to produce and manufacture things; (ii) technologies of sign systems, which allow us to communicate; (iii) technologies of power, which determine our conduct; and (iv) technologies of the self, which allow us to perform a certain number of operations on our thoughts and bodies so that we can attain a desired level of happiness and sense of fulfilment. According to Foucault (1982c: 225), 'Each [technology] implies certain modes of training and modification of individuals, not only in the sense of acquiring certain skills, but also in the sense of acquiring certain attitudes'.

I distinguish three elements of technologies of communities. The first, which I call the 'programme of meritocracy', refers to the bases and sources of authority in community-founded and -managed FL/OSS projects. I highlight and discuss the different meanings of merit within FL/OSS and the power relations that they signify. I approach this issue by examining relations between volunteer and employed developers, new learners and experienced community members, and programmers and non-programmers. In each case I highlight how specific perceptions, priorities and practices come together to privilege certain forms of knowledge and practice over others. At the same time, I consider the tensions and points of balance that can be observed in each of these pairs of relations as symptomatic of the broader challenges FL/OSS communities face in mobilizing and organizing participation as they grow and consolidate their links with the market economy.

The second element of technologies of communities relates to the invocation of the idea of community as a strategy for mobilizing action and maintaining a common basis of participation. As I show, the notion of 'community' in the context of an open, online collective does not have a given meaning. I argue that the invocation of the idea of community is related to specific types of performance by individuals and groups, designed to uphold the positive social values associated with FL/OSS and maintain a common basis of participation.[5] These performances are both ritualistic and strategic. They are rituals in that they help affirm important shared values, such as the importance of user feedback, a culture of sharing and reciprocity, and the idea that every contribution is important, no matter how small. They are strategic in that they can express specific agendas and interests and they help position the actors relative to one another.

The third element of technologies of communities concerns the tools and techniques for community management. I make the point that the different tools that FL/OSS projects use in order to coordinate production—such as mailing lists, websites, wikis—are not merely means to an end, but have a crucial role in making concrete the shared space of collaboration, enabling the actors to participate. Thus, they can be used for coordination, study and appropriation.

RELATIONAL POWER AND CONSTELLATIONS
OF PRACTICE: THE TRANSFORMATION AND
TRANSFORMATIVE POTENTIAL OF FL/OSS

When the different components of my conceptual toolbox are assembled they form a framework that conveys a particular view of FL/OSS communities and the model of FL/OSS organization. In this book I consider FL/OSS communities as constellations of practice that are embedded in existing market dynamics and monetary flows.[6] The character and skills of the different CoP that collaborate in the context of FL/OSS communities will depend on the knowledge domains of the various projects and their degrees of commercialization. I hypothesize that in commercialized communities, relations between volunteers and employed contributors will form an important aspect of participation and the division of labour. I expect that the make-up of the constellations of practice will vary according to the particular audiences of FL/OSS projects. Projects that address the needs of specialized audiences, such as scientists, educators, health professionals and also those of the general public, will need to engage experts and individuals interested in improving the overall user experience and quality of the software. This perspective adds another dimension to the study of the division of labour in FL/OSS and invites us to reconsider existing models that focus exclusively on programming tasks. A third aspect of the division of labour discussed in this book relates to the process of socialization of new programmers. My aim here is to rebalance oversocialized accounts of learning by studying more closely issues related to access and control.

In this book I propose another lens through which the FL/OSS model of cooperation can be examined that adds a further layer of complexity to the view of FL/OSS projects as constellations of practice that are embedded in market flows. This lens draws on Foucault's ideas about the relational, historical character of power to examine critically the idea that the FL/OSS model expresses a paradigm shift in the organization of production. His approach to studying power relations invites us to peel back the layers of meaning in the social character of FL/OSS development and to identify the rules, processes and practices that support specific definitions of merit and status. His emphasis on the relational nature of power reveals the ambiguous character of the interpenetration of social and economic relations. Firms deciding to benefit from FL/OSS often depend on volunteer contributions; companies wanting to initiate their own FL/OSS projects must not appear overpowering or they will fail to invite external contributions. And those with vested interests in community-driven FL/OSS projects must be subtle in their interventions if they are not to alienate the

FL/OSS community. At the same time, Foucault's ideas on how different paradigms of power evolve prompt us to consider the broader implications of the FL/OSS model of organization as a dialogue between the dynamics of change and appropriation. I use the Foucauldian definition of technology to organize the different elements that render the FL/OSS paradigm of collaboration distinctive. The different elements of technologies of communities encapsulate the means through which FL/OSS communities are constructed and the tools and techniques they use in order to invite and retain their members.

The next four chapters explore different aspect of this framework. In Chapter 3, I examine the complexity of the methodological issues arising from the study of FL/OSS communities and how researchers, business people and FL/OSS practitioners attempt to understand and control a process that is largely decentralized. Analysis of the data generated through the development process and community life is central to this undertaking and highlights the importance of the third element of technologies of communities: the online tools that help to make concrete the shared space of collaboration.

In Chapter 4, I focus on how FL/OSS is used as part of an array of business strategies, how firms contribute in FL/OSS development and why they are interested in cultivating communities around their products. This part of the discussion contributes to the understanding of the embedded character of FL/OSS and highlights the challenges firms face in mobilizing volunteer contributions. It also directs attention to the conditions that need to be in place for the idea of community to be effectively invoked.

I point to the implications of commercialization for community-initiated and -driven projects in Chapter 5. Here the nature of commercial contributions in a context in which firms have less control over the development process than in the cases of FL/OSS projects that they themselves initiate is highlighted. This chapter provides insights on how companies and communities negotiate and align their priorities and interests, and directs attention to the special role of employed programmers.

Issues of peripheral participation are the focus of Chapter 6, where the barriers to access for new contributors and the motives and character of the teams that perform non-programming tasks are discussed. These findings challenge established ideas about the character of meritocracy and the experience of peripherality. After approaching the FL/OSS phenomenon from different perspectives, I bring together the insights and findings in Chapter 7 to draw some conclusions about the evolution and transformative potential of FL/OSS as a new model of production. In Chapter 8 I focus on the wider implications of these developments for the evolution of the relationship between sociality and economic production.

3 FL/OSS as an Object of Research
Methodological and Disciplinary Issues

FL/OSS development generates an endless stream of publicly accessible data. Changes to the software are organized and recorded through the use of online tools that help manage the contributions of dozens—and, in some cases, hundreds—of developers. Debates and discussions are recorded on publicly accessible mailing lists. Developers express their views and give an account of their activities on personal blogs. The public image of large-scale projects is communicated through their official web pages which provide detailed information on the rules and norms of participation. Smaller projects are hosted on FL/OSS project foundries which provide aggregate data on the activity of projects they host. Curiosity about the motives of FL/OSS developers has spurred numerous studies, including a number of large-scale online surveys.

Despite this wealth of data, it is almost impossible to answer such simple questions as how many FL/OSS projects are active at a given time or what are the characteristics of a representative FL/OSS project. If we were to define representativeness on the basis of the most frequent characteristics in a given population, for example, then the most representative project in SourceForge, one of the largest FL/OSS project repositories,[1] would be one that included a handful of developers and rarely reached a mature stage of development (Krishnamurthy, 2002; Rainer and Gale, 2005). In other words, attributes that conform to the established conception of FL/OSS projects, such as community development, do not apply to a large number of FL/OSS initiatives and carry different meanings when applied to firm-initiated or grassroots FL/OSS initiatives. Basing our definition of FL/OSS on specific attributes, such as community development, may widen or narrow the perspective and change what is seen as belonging to this area of investigation.

Methodological considerations appear somewhat superfluous in view of the fundamental questions that remain unanswered in relation to cooperation, organization and governance. Issues such as how a population of FL/OSS projects is defined and on what basis analytical representativeness is established, usually form the backdrop to the study of more captivating subjects. As a result, these are rarely discussed in depth outside expert circles. In this chapter, however, these issues take centre stage. Methodological issues are important because they are integral to an assessment of the validity and generalizability of empirical findings. Equally, they are connected to the types of questions we can ask and the way FL/OSS is perceived and taken up in business and policy. More importantly, their consideration reveals that the study of FL/OSS development is as much about constructing an object of research as analysing it. The wealth of available data should not direct attention away from the fact that the process of recovering a coherent view of community through the fragments of development and social life is necessarily biased. Some of these issues raise important ethical questions about privacy and the relations between research and practice.

HUNTING FOR THE—ELUSIVE—PROFILE OF FL/OSS CONTRIBUTORS

Early attempts to explain the success of the FL/OSS movement were dominated by 'insider', practitioner and journalistic accounts which emphasized its critical and subversive character, compared to existing approaches to software development, and the uniqueness of its supportive organizational and legal framework (Linus and Diamond, 2001; Moody, 2001; Raymond, 2001). Although altruism and the private provision of public goods is not new in economics (Arrow, 1972; Titmuss, 1971), excitement over the scaling potential of volunteer production supported by new technology has intensified interest in FL/OSS as a new mode of production (Benkler, 2006).

Early academic research on FL/OSS was driven by the desire to decipher a phenomenon that was often conceived as involving individuals working without obvious pecuniary benefit on projects to produce outputs that were freely available to others. Research sought to find out who these individuals were and why they contributed to these initiatives. FL/OSS contributors did not conform to any obvious economic model, and for those who remain committed to pecuniary motivations, FL/OSS remains unfathomable.

The first systematic, empirical investigations of FL/OSS featured a small number of influential, large-scale surveys that attempted to map the terrain of FL/OSS development by identifying the socio-economic profiles and motivations of developers across many different projects (David et al., 2003; Ghosh et al., 2002; Lakhani and Wolf, 2005). Interest in deciphering contributor motivations has also guided numerous investigations that focus on the developer populations of specific, successful FL/OSS projects (Hertel et al., 2003; Roberts et al., 2006). Some of these initial studies address some (mis)conceptions about developers, related to the image of the rebel 'hacker in the bedroom', and reveal the extent to which project performance and leadership depend on seasoned information technology professionals and not on students or hobbyists (Ghosh, 2005). But the question of who participates in FL/OSS development and why they do so continues to be the focus of investigation. This to some extent is due to the evolution of FL/OSS and its transformation into a mainstream phenomenon.

The growing involvement of companies in volunteer developer communities is expected to change the structure of motivation and participation. This has generated interest in investigating whether and how the commercialization of FL/OSS is affecting volunteer participation. Equally important, the evidence still does not 'add up'; it is not clear whether volunteer FL/OSS developers continue to be driven primarily by the desire to learn or the enjoyment derived from solving problems, or by the prospect of a (better) paid job. The insights that have accumulated since 2003—partly as a result of large-scale surveys—highlight the limitations of the approaches adopted so far in clarifying the profile of FL/OSS contributors. These include the challenge of establishing representativeness when very little is known about the wider population from which a sample is drawn, the inherent weakness of surveys as data collection instruments, and the assumptions made about contributors that guide questionnaire design and data analysis. A broader set of issues concerns the conditions under which examinations of developer motivations can be fruitful and the question of whether a given observation about contributor motivation can be generalized as an explanation of FL/OSS participation.

Take first the issue of representativeness. There has been much debate over the highly skewed samples of large-scale, web-based surveys which arise largely from self-selection by respondents. In the widely influential FL/OSS survey (Ghosh et al., 2002), for example, 68% of respondents were involved in small, immature projects (Ghosh, 2005)—which might indeed be representative of the wider project FL/OSS population, at least in strictly numerical terms. This highlights the importance of establishing what constitutes the FL/OSS model of development and how a population of projects and developers is defined. Do we include in this model volunteer as well as commercially funded projects? Do we include projects initiated by schools and universities? Do we include projects that scale and projects that do not? Is a census of FL/OSS projects meaningful given that only a small percentage attracts a community large and diverse enough to initiate a virtuous cycle between participation and contribution that underlies the bazaar style of development?[2]

The limitations of survey data are well documented in the social science literature (Bertrand and Mullainathan, 2001; Tanur, 1992) and include the subjective nature of responses, the cognitive effects of how questions are worded and the difficulties involved in measuring attitudes that may or may not exist in a coherent form. An additional factor in a movement such as FL/OSS is the extent to which responses are shaped by the cultural image portrayed by the writings on the values of the hacker ethic (Himanen, 2001) and popular accounts of the utility, performance and novelty of FL/OSS (Raymond, 2001). Survey questions often reproduce these assumptions (Tanur, 1992) by adopting popular premises, leaving little room for the discovery of new ideas and associations. This limitation applies to many studies of developer motivations.

Some of the earliest studies assume an opposition between intrinsic and extrinsic developer motivations. Intrinsic motivations are associated with activities that satisfy basic psychological needs such as enjoyment, competence and control. In the case of FL/OSS developers, intrinsic motivations include the joy derived from problem solving and learning and the satisfaction that derives from contributing to a public good (Lakhani and Wolf, 2005). Extrinsic motivations are related to needs such as peer recognition and material and monetary rewards.[3]

Such categorizations can lead to reductive explanations that hide more than they reveal. For example, consider the idea that many FL/OSS developers contribute because 'it's fun'. What exactly does this mean? Are all aspects of contribution 'fun'? Is it 'fun' when people do not respond to queries, or when contributors engage in flame wars and programmers are arrogant or dismissive of others' efforts? Are all aspects of programming 'fun'? One study (Shah, 2006) indicates that long-term volunteers often undertake the more boring, maintenance-related tasks of development which can hardly be described as fun. Admittedly, there are many aspects of FL/OSS that appeal to people's creativity. But unless we delve more deeply into how people's expectations and interests are realized and sustained, there is a danger that previous explanations will be reiterated with little critical assessment.

The model of opposition between intrinsic and extrinsic motivations has been revised considerably. Researchers are adopting more elaborate behavioural models that take account of more parameters of participation. One study of the Apache project examines the association between different clusters of motivations that resulted from the relative importance of different types of contributions and varying levels of participation (Roberts et al., 2006). The results are intriguing and reveal that status aspirations enhance the strength of intrinsic motivation. Moreover, being paid to contribute is positively associated with status motivations. Employed developers are keener to make a name for themselves than volunteers and contributors who are more interested in the use value of the software (meaning that they are interested in addressing a fault or adding a feature that is relevant for them). Moreover, rather surprisingly, satisfaction and the joy of programming are not associated with performance. Volunteers who are driven by their love for the project and programming or are motivated by use value are not regular contributors.

Another interesting, interview-based study which compares contributor motivations around a project initiated and controlled by a firm and one that evolved around a volunteer, grassroots-initiated and -managed community points to an evolution of motivations over time. The study highlights differences between volunteers working in grassroots FL/OSS communities and in commercially initiated projects where changes to the source code are controlled by the firm (Shah, 2006). The findings indicate that similar to employed contributors, most long-term volunteers participating in commercially managed projects become involved in order to meet work-related needs. However, long-standing volunteers in community projects indicate that they are driven primarily by the pleasure of problem solving and creativity and report that they regularly undertake mundane development tasks.

These two studies are indicative of how different dimensions of participation, including the characteristics of projects and the employment status of contributors, may affect the structure of motivations. They build upon a more complex model of behaviour than that premised on a division between intrinsic and extrinsic motivations. They highlight the dynamic character of motives and the way that different aspects of behaviour and participation feed into each other. A student might embark on a career as a FL/OSS developer, then become employed, switch employers or projects, then return to contributing on a voluntary basis. In the process, FL/OSS contributors create networks of connections and attachments that may complement or overlap with existing social circles and professional associations. My study of paid contributors in the GNU Network Object Model Environment (GNOME) and K Desktop Environment (KDE) projects, for example, indicates that employed maintainers, out of a sense of responsibility to the community, often work on parts of the code base that they are not paid directly to contribute to (see Chapter 5). The inconsistency of the results of the two case studies discussed here reveals the problems involved in simply assuming that the FL/OSS terrain is populated by well-established, clearly defined groups of individuals and in not taking account of certain basic project characteristics such as size and character of the user and developer base.

A more refined methodological approach that seeks to go beyond well-established divisions in the FL/OSS developer population is yielding some interesting results. David and Shapiro (2008), for example, re-analysed the FL/OSS survey, weighting responses according to project size. Their findings indicate that larger projects attract what they describe as 'social programmers', that is, older and more experienced contributors, who modify and patch source code to satisfy the needs of their jobs and 'aspiring hackers', who are university graduates keen to develop their skills, whereas small projects are usually 'seeded' by formal student project assignments.

The first large-scale, survey-based investigations of FL/OSS developer profiles and motivations tried to map an unknown terrain. Sampling difficulties, coupled with the limitations of surveys as research instruments and the assumptions made about developers' behaviour, limit the value of the findings. The results hint at, but cannot explore in depth, the multiplicity of the activities and dynamics that are encompassed by FL/OSS. These include reciprocity and commerce, creativity and control, and emergence and design. Later studies that focus on specific project dynamics and draw on interviews, highlight the importance of adopting more elaborate behavioural models to examine interactions among different types of motivations and their evolution over time. The generalizability of these findings is limited, of course, by the specific characteristics of the projects and developer populations investigated.

These insights point to the potentially problematic character of an exclusive focus on motivation as the basis of a full explanation of FL/OSS participation. The search for a profile that describes FL/OSS contributors draws attention to the importance of context. Different project characteristics and dynamics of participation shape frameworks of collaboration that affect the structure of motivation and highlight the need to examine participation in FL/OSS as aspects of professional and learning trajectories.

The multiplicity of FL/OSS projects and the emergence of new configurations of the relationship between private and public add another layer of complexity. Which approaches are appropriate to understand this constantly shifting terrain? The development of empirically and theoretically grounded conceptual models of participation and collaboration based on a better understanding of FL/OSS as a situated phenomenon in private and public life would go a long way towards the development of new insights into the FL/OSS phenomenon.

FL/OSS ORGANIZATION AND COLLABORATION AND PUBLICLY AVAILABLE DATA

FL/OSS development generates many different forms of data that are publicly accessible and which render the process of coordination and collaboration reasonably transparent (von Krogh and Spaeth, 2007). Compared to the unavoidable subjective bias in self-reported survey data, online public data provided through the FL/OSS development and communication infrastructures provide a comparatively accurate and objective record of FL/OSS development. These data have been used extensively as indicators in studies of various aspects of FL/OSS organization and participation. The data vary in terms of content and format (communications, development data, documentation), originate from different sources (VCSs, mailing lists, defects [bug] databases) and reside in different locations (community websites, large software repositories) (Gasser et al., 2004).

Mature FL/OSS projects, such GNOME and KDE, tend to host their own services, whereas immature projects tend to exploit third-party collaboration environments such as the Savannah repository. Large project activities are hosted across a number of online spaces that capture different aspects of community life and development. GNOME and KDE include sites that syndicate content originating from different developer blogs, including, respectively, Planet GNOME and dedicated community news websites such as KDE Dot News. These social and news sites are complemented by a range of resources developed by community members, targeted to different types of audiences (users, developers, sponsors, etc.). They include information for existing and new contributors, guidelines for potential sponsors and community policies related to different aspects of participation and membership such as criteria for the rights to commit to the development tree and conditions for inclusion in higher-level project organizational bodies. Also, established communities usually provide details on the organizational aspects of development, such as how the release process is set up and the roles and responsibilities of actors within the community such as maintainers. Some projects—for example, Debian—even formalize developers' commitments in a form of social contract.[4] These sources of information provide the basis for an expansive and contextual view of FL/OSS development that includes social expressions of participation as well as institutional and technical requirements. These data are frequently exploited in project case studies to situate qualitative and quantitative findings and generate research hypotheses.

These sources of data have some limitations. News sites and blogs provide information that is easily observable but do not constitute the entirety of the communications among participants. Internet Relay Chat (IRC), email, telephone and Voice over Internet Protocol (VoIP) tools—such as Skype—conferences, summits, and face-to-face, one-to-one or small-group meetings enable communication that could be lost to researchers not embedded in the community (and even then it is impossible to be party to all interactions). Project policies and guides are informative, but like other types of rulebooks, they may hide the complexity of the underpinning social arrangements and practices—those that created them and those through which meaning is negotiated and realized.

COMMONLY USED SOURCES OF PUBLIC DATA

The data most commonly analysed are drawn from artefacts and from the communities' principal communication and development tools. They include source code, mailing list archives, defects databases and VCSs, and constitute the barebones FL/OSS infrastructure. A FL/OSS project can run without detailed developer and user documentation, but its decentralized development process cannot be maintained without a VCS tool for tracking changes and managing multiple versions of the software, and a bug database for reporting and managing software defects. Despite the availability of communication tools, such as IRC, my research indicates that mailing lists are indispensable to FL/OSS communities (see Chapter 6). They enable asynchronous participation which is an essential requirement for decentralized, globally distributed development, and they provide a history of conversations in readable format. This history is organized in the form of publicly accessible archives that can be searched and offer essential learning and coordination tools for FL/OSS developer learning and coordination.

Analysis of the data extracted from this minimal set of tools enables comparisons among different FL/OSS projects.

How are these public data used, and what aspects of development and cooperation do they capture in the literature? Due in part to its technically intense character, research employing public data is driven primarily by software engineers. In recent years, a community of researchers, specialized in public data mining and analysis has become established around events such as the International Workshop on Mining Software Repositories.[5] The overview in this chapter draws examples from studies that focus on organizational rather than on purely technical aspects of development.

A potential indicator of the organization of software teams can be derived from a qualitative assessment of the importance of different parts of the code base given on an understanding of the dependencies between its various parts, as indicated by the architectural specifications of the software. In software development, packages usually depend on features and components from several other packages. The mapping of these dependencies helps to establish the relative values of certain modules (Ghosh, 2002). Source code files contain information on other valuable aspects of a projects' organization: in addition to programming language and instructions, they usually include information on authorship and licensing (Robles, 2005).

Information on the relative importance of different software modules and on their authors can be used to create a project hierarchy in which the authors of the most critical parts of the code base—that is, those with the most interdependencies—occupy the highest positions in the social organization. This approach is adopted to examine the network of GNOME and KDE maintainers, the primary source code authors (see Chapter 5) and to analyse patterns of cooperation among these various authors.

In a study by Ghosh and David (2003), authorship information extracted from text files included in the source code is combined with package size and dependencies to examine author productivity. This enables clusters of authorship—that is, teams of developers who worked together on the same packages—to be identified across three versions of the Linux kernel (Ghosh and David, 2003), showing that development occurs in small groups. In another study by Robles, Duenas and González-Barahona (2007), copyright assignments[6] are extracted from Debian source code and used to investigate the evolution of corporate presence over time, in this case indicating that development in FL/OSS was predominantly undertaken by volunteers.

Researchers interested in the evolution of contributions and their authors over time tend to exploit data from VCSs. In contrast to the source code contained in a specific release, which provides a snapshot of work in progress, VCSs, such as the Concurrent Version System (CVS)[7] and Bitkeeper programs, offer a dynamic, historical view of the development process. The data that are extracted, or 'mined', are records or metadata of changes made to the files included in the development tree. These records, taken together, provide a complete history of who made what modifications, to which files and when. In one study (Koch and Schneider, 2002), VCS data mined from the GNOME project revealed that a consistent inner core of developers was responsible for most of the output.

From an organizational point of view, investigating who reports and provides patches for defects and how quickly and successfully highlighted problems are resolved is also important. Mockus, Fielding and Herbsleb (2002) identified Apache's top contributors through version control metadata. Their study also examined the project's bug database and found that it was users from the wider Apache community who submitted the most bug reports. Bug databases are an integral part of a project quality assurance (QA) and coordination process. They organize the reporting of software defects and allow users to request the inclusion of new features in programs. Bug databases allow defects to be categorized according to severity and priority providing the ability to organize discussions focused on specific defects.

Another important set of questions relates to patterns of communication, that is, who are the most frequent communicators, whom do they contact and about what? In FL/OSS development, the primary context for raising and answering questions, discussing and debating, and making announcements is the project mailing lists. The Linux kernel mailing list, for example, reaches almost 300 emails a day.[8] Reading the messages is essential for keeping up to date with new decisions and developments and constitutes a vital learning resource for new developers.[9] Mailing lists are highly socially regulated. Posters are usually advised to keep 'on topic' and submit clear and concise answers which are understandable and can be referred to easily by readers. Decisions or controversies that appear on a community websites are discussed in mailing lists. Large FL/OSS projects may have dozens of lists focusing on different activities and groups. The most important, in terms of traffic and audience, are those that focus on the project's main development activities. These lists act as a collective memory. Robert Love's (2005: 335)[10] view that '[i]f the Linux kernel community had to exist somewhere physically, it would call the Linux Kernel Mailing List home' is reminiscent of Benedict Anderson's (1991) idea of the centrality of certain key texts in nation building.

One approach used in examining patterns of communication focuses on the properties and evolution of the social networks that emerge from email exchanges. At a basic level, the points of such social networks usually represent the individuals that post emails. The lines that link these points usually represent the emails that they exchange. For example, a link between A and B is established when A posts on a mailing list a general query, to which B responds. The intensity and the frequency of email exchanges between developers can be defined and measured in different ways in order to calculate their centrality in the network. A key issue in this type of analysis is who talks to whom, and how frequently, that is, how centralized or decentralized is the network of posters?

Email activity on the Apache http server, in developer mailing lists between 1999 and 2006, indicates a communication network with 'small world' characteristics (Bird et al., 2006). This is a network characterized by a presence of a relatively small group of posters who are responsible for the majority of the email messages it comprises, posters who tend to exchange emails mostly among themselves. The existence of cliques, of closely knit groups of developers, which are relatively stable over time, has been confirmed by studies of the interactions in the principal Linux and KDE mailing lists (Yu et al., 2008). Another interesting dimension of studies of patterns of communication relates to the link between posting behaviour and other types of contributions, such as commits to the development tree. For example, are the people who send the most emails or who receive the most replies also the most active developers (Bird et al., 2006; Yu and Ramaswamy, 2007)? Such studies test the validity of the widely accepted view in FL/OSS that the most active contributors will have the greatest say in the development process and will receive the most attention from their peers.

So far, my review has highlighted the main analytical questions that inform the use of publicly available FL/OSS data from a social science perspective. Interest in social organization has encouraged the use of information contained in source code files to highlight the hierarchy of participation and to reveal patterns of collaboration among the various contributors. Examination of the evolution of both software and contributions—a kind of software 'archaeology'—is supported by data mined from version control repositories which highlight productivity ebbs and flows and demonstrate the persistence or transience of collaboration patterns over time. The structure of communication—who talks to whom and how frequently, another expression of FL/OSS social organization—is investigated through an examination of the patterns of communication visible in the postings made on mailing lists.

There are some questions that cannot be answered through reference to a single artefact and involve interactions or linkages among multiple sources of data. Integration of different sources becomes increasingly necessary as we move from relatively simple questions related to the estimation of effort and productivity, to more complex enquiries into division of labour and patterns of collaboration. There has been a trend towards combining several different data sources in order to recover or reconstruct a layered, multifaceted view of development which its decentralized character tends to fragment. The study by Bird, Gourley, Devanbu, Gertz and Swaminathan (2006), for example, combines data mined from email archives with those obtained through the use of development tools and reveals a strong relationship between email and commit activity. The process of reconstruction is guided by a specific conceptualization of the FL/OSS development process. The view of FL/OSS development as a process of purposive refinement guides a different use of the various data sources to the view of

FL/OSS development as a process of negotiation and contestation. In the first view, attention is directed to the contributions that become part of the main release; in the second, the emphasis is on points of divergence and convergence in different solutions.

The availability of online data does not render them easily analysable in ways that are useful for social scientists (Conklin, 2006). A great deal of work on the data is required before they can be analysed in a meaningful way or combined with other sources. This includes development of methodologies and use of specialized data collection, cleaning, validating and cross-referencing software tools. Some of these issues are worthy of closer examination as they relate to the ability of researchers accurately to capture different aspects of social production.

One such issue is the extent to which these data sources generate accurate, reproducible data. Although some data are generated automatically through the development process, there are often critical aspects that require inputting and updating by developers. These include credit and author files specifying ownership of certain modules, copyright attributions, and so on. This aspect emerges from my analysis of the GNOME and KDE author files, the results of which are presented in subsequent chapters. The GNOME author files included in the official release are reasonably complete, but KDE files are not and require an alternative strategy to identify module ownership. Also, the irregularity of information updates across different modules, indicated by the dates included in the files, raises questions about which of the community's views they represent.

Another problem with the collection of accurate data concerns the use of automated text processing tools for data extraction, many of which are developed under FL/OSS licences. These tools have evolved from collections of bespoke scripts and include Pyternity and Concentration of Developer Distribution (CODD), used for extracting and analysing authorship information, Mailing List Stats for analysing email boxes, and tools for coordinating data extracted from other tools, such as GlueTheos.[11] Although the use of these tools is unavoidable given the amount of raw data that researchers have to manage, it introduces complexities. There are limits to their accuracy due to differences in the way information is entered—even in files for the same project (Tuomi, 2004). In addition to the manual work that is required to clean and verify data collected in this way, the use of these tools necessitates a documenting of the parameters within which they operate.

There is also an issue about the completeness of the image of development that can be recovered from these sources of information. Are the principal aspects of community life and development mediated through version control repositories, bug databases, certain mailing lists and the source code? Let us consider the source code. The Debian project, in each moment of its development, consists of three different releases: the 'stable' one, which contains the latest officially released code distribution; the 'testing' one, which contains packages that have not yet been accepted as yet into the main release, but are more recent versions of the software; and the 'unstable' one, which is under active development. Each release highlights different dynamics of development and collaboration. Some large projects, such as Apache and GNOME, have evolved into umbrella projects that encompass a multitude of different initiatives and codebases. Although in some cases there are rules that dictate when a project is included in a main distribution, project boundaries can be fuzzy and hard to identify and are often objects of contestation rather than universal acceptance.

Take the example of who can submit code to the development tree. Not every contributor participating in the development process has commit rights. In some projects—for example, Debian—write access to the development tree is highly regulated and involves some form of vetting. Developers are given commit rights only when they have demonstrated capacity and dedication. Until access is granted, their contributions are submitted by other certified developers. This practice is established usually to minimize disruptions to development caused by inexperienced developers and to control the administration of CVS accounts. Similarly, the contributions of non-programming contributors will not be reflected as accurately as those of programmers: from the GNOME and KDE teams, for example, one or two people from each language team usually have the right to commit changes to the development tree. Also, version control or source files do not capture organizational level activity such as participation in foundation work or help with the organization of events.

Finally, insights on collaboration and contribution gained through the use of public data will be limited unless findings are combined with data on basic developer demographics and important milestones in the development process such as the involvement or withdrawal of a company from a project. There has been a tendency—especially among researchers who regard FL/OSS projects as complex systems—to consider projects as self-contained units, in which observed patterns are meaningful in terms of internal project dynamics. Although this approach can provide useful insights, it cannot be used as a basis to explain observed patterns in the development process, such as productivity spikes. The challenge in this scenario is the reverse of the problem of weighting survey responses. It requires data that will enable meaningful distinctions in observed patterns, on the basis of developer profiles such as level of expertise, professional attainment and employment status.

FROM ONE TO MANY: ANOTHER TAKE
ON MAPPING THE FL/OSS TERRAIN

How do we move from a contextualized perspective of FL/OSS development, however varied in depth and detail, to an aggregate, bird's-eye view of the terrain of FL/OSS development, and why is such a view desirable?

Large-scale developer surveys set out to chart the landscape of FL/OSS development from the perspective of individual contributors. Large-scale investigations of FL/OSS are also conducted from the perspective of projects by comparing data from hundreds or even thousands of different projects. Macro examinations serve a variety of purposes. They provide the background required for a general assessment of the model of development and the people driving it. Research has made clear that only a fraction of projects achieve the scalability and technical maturity associated with bazaar-style development. Businessmen and aspiring individuals alike have realized that releasing a project under a FL/OSS licence is not enough to derive the full benefits of volunteer contributions, an aspect of development which, like code maturity, is tied to the notion of a successful community.

In one study, researchers examined the association between licences and the user bases of 40,000 projects hosted on SourceForge (Lerner and Tirole, 2005). They found that projects geared towards end users tend to have restrictive licences, such as the GNU GPL, and that those projects intended for developers or for commercial use tend to have more permissive licences.[12] These findings led the authors to conclude that the choice of licensing method is based on what the licensee is trying to achieve and on the licensee's perception of user community expectations. The authors indicate that commercial projects, compared to grassroots projects, tend to have more restrictive licences in order to deflect suspicions about their ultimate objectives.

Analysis of data mined from FL/OSS code repositories can reveal how specific project attributes may relate to their development characteristics. Data can be derived from the project development tools provided by the software repositories and also gleaned from information available for each project on numbers of registered and active developers, key contributors, numbers of downloads and releases, licence type, donors, programming language, available translations, and so on. In several cases, forges provide statistics on the project development cycles that allow existing and potential contributors to assess the vitality of and the prospects for further development. Forges offer a wealth of data for testing research hypotheses on the factors and combinations of factors that affect the evolution of projects, from both technical and communal perspectives. A line of research that is carried over from case studies focuses on the organization of collaboration, that is, the degree to which different aspects of development are decentralized or centralized. Examination of this issue across hundreds of projects can help to decipher the different 'flavours' and lifecycles of social production by highlighting differences and commonalities across large project populations.

In a study of 140 projects hosted on SourceForge, researchers analysed developer emails on bugs (Crowston and Howison, 2005).[13] The results indicate the existence of a few highly centralized projects in which the majority of the email exchanges involve a few people, and a few decentralized projects, in which individuals exchange emails with many different contributors. The degree of centralization of the majority of projects examined lies somewhere between these two extremes. This led to the conclusion that, despite the popular view, FL/OSS projects are not characterized by a particular social structure. Another investigation (Capiluppi and Milchmayr, 2007), however, suggests that project structure might be a function of evolution, with some projects going through an initial, centralized, 'cathedral' phase at the beginning of development before evolving into full-fledged bazaars. Investigations of these and other project attributes contribute to the development of typologies and classifications aimed at highlighting the factors at the heart of the complexity and diversity of FL/OSS.

However, macro-level studies are valuable not just because they provide a means of contextualizing FL/OSS success stories offering a sounder basis for generalization, but also because they include questions that cannot be answered through project-centred studies. FL/OSS developers, for example, frequently participate in more than one project and move between projects. The allocation of effort among projects is crucial for the sustainability of FL/OSS software. Investigating the bigger picture can provide valuable insights on the relationships between the FL/OSS movement, the software industry and the policy sector by posing questions about which areas are most intensively developed, which ones lag behind proprietary solutions and how employment affects recruitment in FL/OSS projects.

The growing integration of FL/OSS software in commercial and public products, systems and services creates a need for criteria to assess the quality and maturity of the FL/OSS projects that are considered for adoption. This is making macro-level FL/OSS research increasingly attractive to the commercial sector. Public and private actors, sometimes with the cooperation of FL/OSS communities, are expending effort on developing methodologies to produce reliable indicators for evaluating the suitability of FL/OSS for use at the organizational level and in mission critical environments. An initiative aimed at providing benchmark tools for businesses and policy makers is the Software Quality Observatory (SQO-OSS) which is a consortium of FL/OSS projects, consultants and public research institutions that is working on a methodology to evaluate quality projects, based on indicators available in FL/OSS project repositories, and maintaining a league-table of FL/OSS applications.[14] A similar framework being developed by Open Business Readiness Rating (OpenBRR) is 'being proposed as a new standard model for rating open source software'.[15]

So what are the challenges underlying macro-level examinations of the FL/OSS terrain? As indicated by the examples cited so far, in most cases the sampling frame is provided by the collaborative software development environment hosting the selected projects, of which SourceForge is by far the most popular. However, Freshmeat.org and GNU Savannah, two other major software repositories, also host projects that are part of official GNU software and which run on free operating systems. There are a few more focused repositories that are organized on the basis of programming languages, such as RubyForge and JavaForge, or were initiated and are managed by prominent companies. For example, Microsoft established Codeplex, and Google manages Google code. The terrain is further complicated by the fact that major FL/OSS projects, such as Apache and Linux, are not hosted on forges, but rely on their own infrastructure.

This multiplicity of collaborative spaces creates important challenges for the collection of comparable data on the population of FL/OSS projects and their developers. The merits of a FL/OSS project census are debatable given the large number of initiatives that are introduced as 'pet' or school projects and never take off. Even if inactive projects were to be categorized as 'noise' and excluded from the outset, there are still multiple sampling and data collection issues, and numerous spaces and projects that would evade examination. Should sponsored projects with an existing code base be considered on the same basis as grassroots, bootstrap initiatives? How should developers working across projects hosted on different sites be classified in terms of their affiliations?

The two main methods used to collect comparable FL/OSS data are data dumps and spidering or crawling (Howison et al., 2006). Data dumps are databases on projects hosted in the same collaborative environment that are grouped together in the form of tables. They are used by forges to store project management activity and statistics. Among the problems involved in accessing these data are the cost of the databases, the changes required to enable academic analysis, such as anonymizing contributors, and the difficulties involved in interpreting the schema or categories of data and the meaning of the relationships between them. A further complication is that not all forges make their databases available for research.

Spidering or crawling involves the use of sets of scripts to systematically browse websites and extract relevant data. The process is enabled by the fact that individual project websites in a repository are generated on the basis of a common HTML template. This means they include the same types of information (project name, licence, programming language, type of project, etc.), organized in similar ways. This data collection method is technically demanding and requires a number of steps before data can be summarized and presented in a format that is appropriate for analysis. Some forges restrict spidering because of the bandwidth burden that the process imposes on sites and have specific guidelines related to data collection.[16] The difficulties involved in preparing public FL/OSS data for academic analysis have led to a number of initiatives that provide prepared data sets, including Notre Dame University's SourceForge, net data dumps[17] and Flossmole, which provides up-to-date data sets from five different forges (Howison et al., 2006). Different schemes for naming and identifying data also add complexity to comparisons across different projects. Finally, different FL/OSS tools, such as VCSs and bug databases, provide slightly different information.

Semantics are important in this context for another reason. The use of common ideas and notions in FL/OSS communities often belies important differences in meaning and realization within each project. The meaning ascribed to the role of 'maintainer' is tied to a project's history, for example, and to the way a community chooses to express rights and responsibilities and formalize admission criteria for its core membership. Notions of what constitutes a substantive contribution and how different sorts of membership are defined are evolving and are also frequently contested.[18] There are also great disparities in how authorship and credit are defined, verified and claimed or endowed. Some projects, for example, discourage people from claiming credit directly in the source code files. Thus, context plays an important role in data interpretation and locating sources of information. This loss of context has more far-reaching implications than those associated with the normal offsets that are seen to characterize large-scale quantitative examinations.

NEW DIRECTIONS AND UNDER-EXPLOITED OPPORTUNITIES

Notwithstanding the difficulties involved in extracting and normalizing, cleaning and combining raw data, public sources of FL/OSS information for research suffer from yet another weakness. The attributes available for study are limited and do not cover all the aspects of the projects that are of interest to researchers. Forges are built around projects, not developers, and provide little information on the interactions among different projects and developers. This to some extent may be changing. It has been suggested that the design of new forges should incorporate features that allow multiple views of projects, developers and organizations participating in FL/OSS (González-Barahona et al., 2008). This would facilitate the grouping of contributions and projects included in the same distributions—those developed by companies, by the same individuals or groups of individuals, and so on.

What else is missing from this overview of popular research designs and data sources employed in examining FL/OSS development? The three most popular examination vantage points presented are the developer (in surveys), the project (in case studies) and the forge (in cross-project investigations). Studies of companies participating in FL/OSS generally are scarce. However, as firm experimentation with FL/OSS is increasing, so is its study. This redirects the focus to access by people and of places. Another area that has escaped researchers' attention is the role of emerging FL/OSS institutions. The contributions of the FSF and the Open Source Foundation in shaping the institutional and legal frameworks of FL/OSS development are well established. However, the roles of these institutions in standards, and their broader role in coalescing and dividing parts of the FL/OSS community, have yet to be systematically investigated.

Little research exists on offline aspects of FL/OSS, such as community events and meetings. A cursory scanning of mailing lists and community pages shows that there are numerous gatherings of different levels of formality and with different aims. FL/OSS development is punctuated by local get-togethers, annual project development meetings (GNOME, Boston summit) and community events (KDE akademy, GNOME Users and Developers European Conference [GUADEC]), sub-project meetings, pan-European gatherings (Free and Open Source Software Development European Meeting [FOSDEM], Linux Tag) and global events (Global Open Source Conference).

ETHICS AND VALUES

The development of FL/OSS metrics is becoming a business. Ohloh is a company that specializes in generating easily interpretable FL/OSS project and developer statistics. A subscription fee allows developers to evaluate the viability and maturity of various projects and to choose which projects are commonly combined by users in order to publicize their own projects and to track the contributions of other developers. This last aspect has led to discussions on whether such services and related research may breach contributors' privacy or misrepresent their work. Would John, for example, want to reveal that he had not committed any changes in a five-month period despite the noise he has created on mailing lists? And what might be the reaction of Bob's boss to finding that Bob had been working intensively on a FL/OSS project while lagging in what he needs to deliver in his job?

Mathias Hasselman, a GNOME contributor, has the following to say:

> I don't want anyone to do statistics about FOSS contributions. Those stats make me feel naked . . .
>
> Also I do not like the stats at ohloh.net, because they draw a very incomplete picture of my FOSS contributions, when you search for my real name. The only way to change this, is registering at ohloh.net, and associat[ing] all my shell accounts. I don't want to register at any random web community, just to force them to publish accurate information about me. I don't want this, as it costs my time, and I don't want this, as it restricts my freedom by accepting their terms of use.
>
> What makes people believe they are allowed to do such stats? Simply the fact, that this information is available without much effort? Drastically spoken, it's also not much effort to break into houses, or to commit homicide—does the little effort make this actions legal?[19]

This posting generated numerous responses. Some people suggested that the developers who had chosen to use their real names could rectify the situation by assuming a pseudonym. Others focused on potential infringement(s) to the law incurred by compiling information on individuals from online sources; some considered this to be an unavoidable consequence of the transparency of FL/OSS projects.

Developer-related statistics are frequently produced in the context of individual projects. The KDE community, for example, regularly posts lists of top-tier contributors and bug fixers in its newsletters, and Cia.vc, a free online service, has been providing updated information on project development obtained via VCSs since 2003. In 2001 Google released hackystat, 'an open source framework for collection, analysis, visualization, interpretation, annotation, and dissemination of software development process and product data'.[20] The project has had many releases since then.

The need to compile, visualize and interpret information on FL/OSS communities is driven by various actors: researchers who are interested in learning more about FL/OSS as a software development and organizational process; individuals and organizations who are interested in using FL/OSS software and participating in community development; and FL/OSS practitioners. Although FL/OSS communities have developed effective practices and processes for addressing some of challenges (such as time-based releases) posed by asynchronous, distributed development that relies largely on a volatile, volunteer labour force, there are a number of issues that cannot be addressed effectively without a composite view of development, which can be shared among participants. The combination of different sources of information can contribute to a meaningful, holistic view of development and can provide a basis for reflection as well as action. Pinpointing areas of development or specific bugs that seem not to be receiving attention may help to address crucial QA issues and become an important tool for mobilizing and steering participation. Visualization of contributor networks might provide insights that could result in new collaborations or inform important policy and governance decisions. For example, what are the implications of rendering visible the importance of the contributions and areas of work of paid contributors?

Metrics also encompasses another dimension to which Matthias's blog entry alludes, namely, its implications for meritocracy. As previously mentioned, the positions of individuals in FL/OSS communities in the social organization is influenced by the quantity and quality of their contributions. There are several advantages to an objective grounding to this hierarchy, because this may minimize the influence of those contributors who have little to offer or who consistently undermine a project. There are also disadvantages. As well as considering how meaningful the metrics related to code contributions are and how they are obtained, we need to consider more broadly how they affect the definition of merit. Some aspects of contributions are hard to quantify, based either on their nature or technical and administrative constraints. How should we assess the value of the contributions made by artists or those involved in advocacy, or those who provide support to new users and developers?

Despite these limitations, FL/OSS communities are more transparent than other types of collective endeavour—and certainly more so than software teams operating in proprietary contexts. The possibilities for utilizing the data generated through the software development practices and processes of community development offer researchers and practitioners unique opportunities for understanding their coordination and highlighting the value of the notion of 'technologies of communities'. As indicated earlier in this chapter, however, the costs associated with reconstituting meaning from the interpretation of raw public FL/OSS data are not insubstantial. The meanings that emerge are incomplete and cannot be perceived as being entirely objective.

There remains the question of whether it is appropriate for researchers to try to penetrate spaces that might be considered by some FL/OSS contributors to be private. Mapping, after all, is a political act: it aims to fix what is elusive, to name and categorize what exists only in the imagination. As is indicated by commercially oriented open source metrics, mapping is akin to appropriation. It is thus an integral part of the transformation of FL/OSS into a mainstream phenomenon. It also reflects wider trends regarding the development of computational social science, a branch of social science that involves the analysis of massive amounts of data generated through online transactions (Lazer et al., 2009).

We should also consider what such increased visibility and possibilities for control and agency entailed in these acts of measurement and mapping mean for a culture that identifies itself as 'a deep-rooted critical mentality and willingness to challenge, confront, and build alternatives to deep-rooted social, educational, political and economic institutions' (Hill, 2002: 2).[21] Although some individuals interested in mapping the FL/OSS space and its contributors are committed to the form of open investigation espoused by the FL/OSS community, others may not share the academic and FL/OSS communities' values of transparency and freedom of information. And let us not forget that, despite the existence of norms that regulate how personal data are collected and used, some of the ethical issues raised in this new context are also terra incognita for social science. Although it is impossible to put the genie back in the bottle, it is necessary to keep engaging in public debate about the relationship between norms and regulations that is necessary to maintain a balance between the desire to study and learn and to profit from personal data when it may infringe individual rights to privacy.

4 Commercial Involvement and FL/OSS

FL/OSS occupies a space in public imagination where emergent forms of collaboration supported by ICTs question the efficiency of traditional forms of organization. The relationships between the old and the new, the ingrained and the radical, take many forms and are expressed in differing terms. An initial emphasis on the opposition in the values of the gift and the exchange economies, for example, has given way to accounts of hybridity, interest in emerging institutions, mixed models of public and private innovation, and a concern for how best to manage the relations between firms and volunteers (Goldman and Gabriel, 2005; Lessig, 2008; von Hippel and von Krogh, 2003). The involvement of firms in FL/OSS development is increasing, not just through co-production or participation in community initiated and governed FL/OSS projects, but also in terms of initiating FL/OSS projects.

The popularity of FL/OSS development comes at a price. Practitioners point to the confusion over what FL/OSS is and over the practices and norms of the social process underlying the FL/OSS model of development which form part of the horizon of expectations of its volunteer contributors. Volunteers' perceptions of FL/OSS are often counterbalanced by commercial experimentation with different models of appropriation and control over the outputs and the processes of development. There is a study that indicates that long-established FL/OSS norms, such as the notion of community governance models, are becoming decoupled from the idea of FL/OSS projects (O'Mahony, 2007). Nevertheless, as indicated by the many unsuccessful attempts to appropriate the benefits of FL/OSS, there are limits to what can be achieved without reference to volunteers' concerns and values.

The commercial adoption of FL/OSS and corporate involvement in communal models of software development are regarded frequently as constitutive of a company's 'open source strategy'. A key concept in analysing the commercial adoption of FL/OSS is the idea of the business model, the 'revenue architecture' for capturing the value from technology. Although the idea of a business model as the central expression of a firm's open source strategy may be useful in certain contexts, it can also be misleading. It is debatable whether companies have consistent FL/OSS strategies and whether all aspects of their uses of FL/OSS are part of these strategies. Also, accounts centred around the idea of a business model fail to capture the spill-over benefits of firm engagement in FL/OSS development, including learning in the context of communities of practice and at the level of the organization. This chapter develops a basic taxonomy of commercial involvement in FL/OSS development that takes account of the different dimensions of commercial strategies and practice. It supports the argument that the relationships between FL/OSS and the commercial world should be considered on the basis of the difference between 'institution' and 'collaboration' (Shirky, 2005), but also as part of an ongoing effort to manage the relation between 'private' and 'public' and seeing volunteer communities as distinct spaces of economic production.

COMMERCIAL CONTRIBUTION IN FL/OSS COMMUNITIES

How do companies support FL/OSS development? Established FL/OSS institutions, such as the FSF, which receive donations from individuals, also receive money from various corporate and business programmes. And non-profit organizations, which help to manage community relationships with external actors, such as the Apache and GNOME Foundations, have created similar programmes that are successful in attracting funding. Commercial support also comes in the form of providing important services to the FL/OSS community. In 2005, Open Source Development Labs, a consortium of leading industry players including International Business Machines Corporation (IBM), Intel and Hewlett Packard (HP),[1] donated US$ 4 million to create the Software Freedom Law Center which provides 'legal representation and law-related services to protect and advance FL/OSS'.[2]

Companies support consortia and other initiatives aimed at promoting the wider adoption of FL/OSS and stimulating participation in FL/OSS development. In 2008, HP, in cooperation with the Linux Foundation and several companies including Google and Novell Inc., launched a project called FOSSBazaar. This is an open community initiative that focuses on the issues of open source governance and aims to help 'companies address the legal, financial and security risks faced when adopting free and open source software'.[3] Since 2005, Google has been running the annual competition, 'The Google Summer of Code', which awards monetary prizes to students who successfully complete small-scale FL/OSS projects for established FL/OSS communities.

Firms also contribute by donating proprietary code as a one-off gesture to increase the functionality of existing FL/OSS projects, or by submitting modifications to original code to the main development tree, to suit their own purposes. In general, community-founded and -managed FL/OSS projects welcome such contributions, but use the same criteria to decide about their inclusion as are applied to judge the work of volunteers. Some firms donate bandwidth (to enable faster download and access to the development tree), donate hardware (such as computers for developers, workstations for testing builds, devices and graphics cards for testing device drivers, etc.), sponsor the organization of community events and provide network services. They may provide expertise in areas where FL/OSS developers lack certain skills. Sun Microsystems Inc., for example, helped the GNOME community to modify its accessibility framework through the incorporation of features in the software that allow people with disabilities to use it more easily.

Firms can also donate software programs and tools to the volunteer community by releasing them under OSI-compliant[4] or free software licences. In 2006 IBM donated e-learning software code to the Sakai Project, a group of learning institutions creating and deploying open source course management, collaboration and online research support tools for higher education.[5] Somewhat more controversial is support provided in the form of pledges and commitments made by companies, universities or not-for-profit organizations that they will not invoke specific patents against the FL/OSS community.[6] Some consider such pledges to be ineffective because they are often limited to certain projects and do not preclude the patents from being invoked at some future time. Others argue that pledges may be problematic—especially if the conditions applying to the rights being transferred to the public are not sufficiently detailed or clear[7] and if the same corporation making the pledge is simultaneously lobbying for stronger patent control.

Some firms release entire proprietary programs under FL/OSS licences. IBM's Eclipse, a popular software development platform, Sun Microsystems Inc.'s programming language Java, and the OpenOffice.org productivity suite are well-known examples of proprietary programs that have evolved into sponsored FL/OSS projects, each with its own developer community. And governments, education and research institutions, and regional and local authorities release code in free software licences or under OSI compliant licences in the hope of attracting volunteer contributions. The reasons for these initiatives and the dynamics of participation in these 'synthetic'[8] FL/OSS projects are considered in more detail in the subsequent parts of this chapter.

EXAMINING THE BUSINESS ECOLOGY OF A GRASSROOTS FL/OSS PROJECT

A form of sponsorship that is attracting attention (Dahlander and Wallin, 2006; Henkel, 2008) is the involvement of firm employees in FL/OSS community-initiated and -managed software projects. An examination of the business ecology of two such projects, GNOME and KDE, is a good starting point for understanding the various business strategies and practices in FL/OSS. The advantages of these forms of involvement are considered in depth in Chapter 5, which deals with the issue of firm employed community members.

Tables 4.1 and 4.2 provide details on numbers of organization sponsored contributors in the GNOME Foundation and KDE e.V. The GNOME Foundation and KDE e.V. are non-profit organizations that coordinate the efforts of FL/OSS communities, provide help with legal and financial matters, and help to manage relations with firms. Membership in GNOME and KDE is regulated and based on a verifiable record of contributions. This means that their members include some of the more active and committed contributors.[9]

The data were gathered mainly through an email survey conducted in the summer of 2006 which yielded 199 responses from GNOME Foundation members (59.4% response rate) and 63 from KDE e.V. members (55.7% response rate). I focused on GNOME and KDE because I wanted to examine how commercialization affects cooperation in the context of two mature FL/OSS communities that share the same objective, in this case, the development of a Graphical User Interface (GUI) environment for Unix.[10] The survey was part of a larger study that included interviews with a large number of GNOME and KDE contributors and observations conducted in numerous community events. Comparisons between the two projects yield some interesting insights that are presented as my account unfolds.

Table 4.1 Organizations Employing Members of KDE e.V.

Organization	No. of organizations	No. of employees	Total employees
Novell Inc./SUSE	1	5	5
Self-employed/Sub-contracting work	1	4	4
Klarälvdalens Datakonsult AB, Trolltech ASA	2	3	6
Basyskom GmbH, Credativ GmbH,Froglogic GmbH, Intel Corporation, Linspire Inc., Linupfront GmbH, Linux4MEDIA GmbH, Mandriva Labs-Brazil, Re/Source Inc., RedHat Inc., Sirius Corporation, Staikos Computer Services Inc, Trolltech ASA & Klarälvdalens Datakonsult AB, University of Nijmegen	14	1	14
Total			29

Source: KDE e.V. Survey, N=63

Table 4.2   Organizations Employing Members of the GNOME Foundation

Organization	No of organizations	No of employees	Total of employees
Novell Inc., Red Hat Inc.	2	16	32
Sun Microsystems Inc.	1	12	12
Self-employed/Subcontracting work	1	8	8
Canonical Ltd	1	4	4
Fluendo SL, Imendio AB, Sharif Farsiweb Inc.	3	3	9
Movial Corporation, Nokia Corporation, Wipro Technologies Ltd	3	2	6
AB Take it, Async Open Source Ltd, Baum Retec AG, Concordia University of Alberta, Golder Software Systems Ltd, Hewlett Packard Inc., Hispafuentes SL, Høgskolen i Agder and Aust-Agder Kulturhistoriske Senter, IBM Corporation,IFIS-Passau, Ildana Teo, Lamdaux-λUX Software services, Mandriva Inc., Molinux, Multitel, OpenedHand Ltd, OpenSource DTP, rPath Inc., Scalix Inc., St-Antonius College Gouda, Sysref, Telsidel, Unitet AS, University of Grenoble 1, University Siegan, Vmware Inc, Vrije Universiteit Amsterdam, WECWild Open Source Inc., X-tend NV	30	1	30
Total			101

Source: GNOME Foundation survey, N=199

The data in Tables 4.1 and 4.2 give information on the number of companies employing GNOME Foundation and KDE e.V. members. Table 4.1 shows that one company, Novell Inc./SUSE, employs five KDE e.V. members and that fourteen companies employ one member each.

Some explanation of the technical characteristics of GNOME and KDE is necessary in order to understand these survey results. Both are multi-level projects providing a desktop environment, a GUI for Unix, together with a collection of end user applications such as office suites, browsers and email clients. In addition, both of the respective communities contribute to the development of the tools used to develop the graphical interface and the applications. Each project, therefore, consists of a number of different components which together form a software stack,[11] which is designed to deliver an end product, such as the GUI, but which can be used also to develop other software. The communities have distinct audiences—an end-user, non-technical audience for the GUI, and a developer audience—which may exploit the tools in the software stack to develop other programs and applications. As I show in Chapter 6, this has implications for the division of labour in these projects.

GTK+ and Qt, respectively, are the graphical user toolkits used by GNOME and KDE and are exploited to develop applications both within and outside the context of the projects. Qt is interesting in that it was developed by a Norwegian-based company, Trolltech ASA, and its initially controversial licensing terms (the licence was incompatible with the redistribution terms set out by FSF and the OSI terms) spurred the creation of the GNOME project. The most prominent sponsors in the GNOME community are Novell Inc. and Red Hat Inc. with 16 contributors each, and Sun Microsystems Inc., with 12. There is also a considerable group of regularly or occasionally subcontracted individuals and a smaller group of firms that occupies the middle range of sponsorship in terms of employment. This includes Canonical Ltd, with four contributors; Fluendo SL and Imendio AB with three; and Movial, the Nokia Corporation and Wipro Ltd with two each. In addition there is a large number of organizations with marginal participation, sponsoring one contributor each. This last group features prominent industry players such as HP and IBM and public organizations such as universities. At the time of the study KDE e.V. included a smaller number of organizations and fewer sponsored contributors than GNOME. The prominent sponsors are Novell Inc. with five developers, and Trolltech ASA and Klarälvdalens Datakonsult AB, with three each. Again, there is an important cluster of self-employed contributors and numerous big corporations with a marginal presence.

How can we begin to understand this ecology? An initial distinction can be made in relation to the types of companies (original size, market focus) that participate in GNOME and KDE. First, there are the insurgents, that is, companies created to commercialize FL/OSS. These FL/OSS-focused start-up companies include large Linux software distributors, such as Red Hat Inc., and smaller, more specialized, software companies, such as Fluendo SL, which specializes in free software multimedia development. Several of these companies are spin-offs from community funded and managed FL/OSS projects. Fluendo SL was created to commercialize Gstreamer, a FL/OSS multimedia platform, and, from its beginnings, has been staffed by programmers who originally were volunteer contributors. Novell Inc.'s core team of open source developers originated in Ximian, a company created by Miguel de Icaza and Nat Friedman, two of the founders of the GNOME project which Novell bought in 2003. Broadly speaking, insurgent FL/OSS companies draw on their expertise in FL/OSS in order to sell complementary services and products. These can include services or extensions to FL/OSS that alleviate some of the costs of adoption, maintenance and integration, thus making them attractive propositions for clients.

Second, there are multinational corporations: hardware, software and systems vendors, such as Sun Microsystems Inc. and IBM, and communication corporations, such as Nokia. These incumbent firms are intensive users and producers of FL/OSS. For example, Nokia's involvement in FL/OSS involves the use of this software in Nokia's handheld devices. Despite its ownership of Symbian OS, a popular, proprietary operating system for mobile devices, Nokia's involvement in FL/OSS development processes has scaled up significantly since 2003. From an initial almost experimental exploitation of a FL/OSS stack that used GTK+ and GNOME in the first model of their Internet Tablet,[12] Nokia created and has maintained Maemo, a FL/OSS platform used to run and develop applications for mobile devices. This development platform is an indication of the willingness of large corporations to experiment with and invest in FL/OSS in ways that can potentially help them to maintain their technological and competitive advantage.

How can we account for the presence of these important sponsors in these communities? Novell Inc.'s presence in both projects is associated with its use of GNOME and KDE as the graphical interface for its Linux distributions. Red Hat Inc. and Canonical Ltd use GNOME as the desktop environment for their shrink-wrapped distributions developed for corporate and individual users. Shrink-wrapped software distributions provide neatly packaged, easy-to-install FL/OSS solutions. Distribution vendors, such as Redhat Inc. and Novell/SUSE Inc., make money from adding value to a set of FL/OSS programs and by selling services that address different client needs. This approach is indicative of the service model of software commoditization. The baseline for adding value rests on the ability to provide convenient, out-of-the-box solutions that bundle together many different programs which are easy to install (desktop distributions come with an install manager and a collection of several different drivers), update and maintain, and which have been tested for seamless working together. A no-frills version of these distributions is usually available for download at no cost.

Revenue in this case is generated by distributors and vendors who customize these distributions for specialized markets and platforms (e.g., for the server and desktop markets, data centres, cloud computing) and by the provision of support services that address the specific needs of customers, such as dealing with legacy software and addressing interoperability in the use of FL/OSS and proprietary systems which help to mitigate some of the risks of FL/OSS adoption. These support services are available through different types of subscriptions and contracts that offer varying levels of support (telephone, 24-hour, on-site, etc.). They may also include specialization, such as the tailoring of software to specific needs which otherwise requires consultancy services.

The service model of software provision, exemplified by the offerings of large Linux distribution vendors, has evolved to address the needs of professionals and business clients interested in building on Linux. Examples of these services include professional certification for software engineers, application packaging and certification for independent software vendors (ISVs), that is, software firms that produce and sell software for different kinds of hardware and operating systems, and hardware certification for hardware manufacturers. Application packaging and certification, such as the SUSE Linux Enterprise ISV Partner Program, guarantees that ISVs' products will work seamless with the vendors' Linux distributions and offer an additional distribution channel.

Another revenue-generating model is based on sales of complements, proprietary add-ons, that are consumed in combination with FL/OSS. One of Fluendo SL's flagship products is proprietary codecs[13] which allow the playback of proprietary media formats on computers that run Linux or another flavour of Unix using Gstreamer. One widely employed revenue-generating model based on FL/OSS is illustrated by the case of Trolltech ASA—one of the contributors to the KDE project—and depends on a dual-licensing strategy. In this case the company releases the software under a copyleft and a commercial licence, the latter involving a licensing fee. The commercial licence allows licensees to use the FL/OSS in the development of their own products without having to comply with the terms of the copyleft licence. A copyleft, OSI-compliant licence requires that any derivative work—that is, any new piece of software that incorporates FL/OSS code—be redistributed in such way that the source code is open and available for redistribution. The commercial licence, therefore, allows companies to incorporate FL/OSS in their products without divulging the code they have developed. Another reason why dual- or even tri-licensing is popular is that it allows licensors and licensees to circumvent some of incompatibilities among different OSI-compliant licences.

A variation of the dual-licensing model which is gaining popularity is the firm strategy of offering two different versions of a product: a copyleft version that provides some basic functionality and a proprietary version that includes a full set of features. Although, in principle, developers can add features to the copyleft version of the program, in practice, this is often very difficult. There is huge controversy over whether this strategy is consistent with the ethos of the FL/OSS community. In 2008 an announcement was made on Slashdot,[14] the most popular FL/OSS news site, that the very popular database MySQL (My Structured Query Language) was close sourcing some parts of its code base. This generated a flurry of comments, which led Sun Microsystems Inc.—the owner of MySQL—to abandon this idea. However, representatives of the company emphasized that Sun would continue to experiment with MySQL's business model.[15]

THE STRATEGIC USE OF FL/OSS IN BUSINESS

So why do companies participate in FL/OSS development? Firms' motivations for contributing to FL/OSS development have been the subject of much study and speculation (Bonaccorsi and Rossi, 2006; Mustonen, 2005; West and Gallagher, 2006). In contrast to individuals' motivations, where the evidence points to the moderation of self-interest by the ideal of reciprocity and the desire to contribute to creating a public good, business motivations are rarely altruistic. Companies are governed by their ownership, whose motives may be diverse, but promoting a strategy that is not aimed at maximizing long-term shareholder value would be hazardous for the management involved. Business altruism is unlikely and rare. In broadening the discussion about the strategic use of FL/OSS in business that was introduced in the previous section, I adopt two analytical perspectives. The first, encapsulated by the idea of complementary assets, draws attention to the conditions, capabilities and skills required to commercialize an innovation (Teece, 1986). Such assets are said to be particularly important in conditions where the nature of the technology and the legal regime is such that, in principle, innovations can be easily understood and imitated. FL/OSS is one such innovation based on availability of the source code and copyleft licensing. The second perspective is useful for understanding FL/OSS as a long-term investment and an instance of organizing the dialogue between the private and public. In this scenario, firm involvement in FL/OSS development is comparable to commercial investment in basic scientific research (Rosenberg, 1989).

Complementary assets include specialized information and distribution channels and services, such as marketing and after-sales support, and different types of know-how and expertise such as engineering efficiency, manufacturing and product design. As we have seen, many business models associated with FL/OSS are based on firms' abilities to deliver whole-product solutions to clients. The service and subscription model of FL/OSS offers a viable alternative to proprietary solutions. This is a characteristic example of how firms add value to FL/OSS by addressing user requirements that FL/OSS developers are not interested in or lack the resources to satisfy.

From this perspective, the entire business model of FL/OSS vendors is built upon the provision of complementary assets, with the core innovation, Linux, and other parts of FL/OSS that make up distributions developed outside the firm boundaries. FL/OSS also plays a central part in strategies that combine proprietary and open elements in order to sell complementary goods that are consumed in combination with other goods and that benefit from the network effects of widely adopted technologies and, subsequently, spur further innovation.

What is the greatest asset of FL/OSS start-up companies? It could be argued that their most valuable asset is their expertise in their particular specialization. Companies such as Ximian, Trolltech ASA and Fluendo SL have always recruited programmers with intensive involvement in the development of the FL/OSS technologies they are seeking to commercialize. As indicated by the number of firm employees participating in the GNOME Foundation and KDE e.V., both incumbents and insurgents involved in FL/OSS development consistently recruit from FL/OSS communities to acquire employees who are knowledgeable in the technology and in the social processes involved in FL/OSS development. In Chapter 5, I consider the implications of this strategy from the perspective of the grassroots communities.

These tacit competencies are important because the ability of companies to generate revenue from FL/OSS is based on continuous improvements to the software which, in turn, depends on the ability to organize and, to some extent, to steer volunteer contributions in a specific direction. The ability to manage relations with volunteers and the reputation for delivery of consistently high-quality products and service have become very important assets for businesses that focus on commercializing FL/OSS. Professional certification schemes that are not backed up by reputation and widely acknowledged expertise are meaningless. In this context, Red Hat Inc.'s aggressive reaction to violations of its trademark, a form of intellectual property right, is not surprising.

FL/OSS is increasingly being used as a distribution channel to disseminate products to a wider technical community (West and O'Mahony, 2008). Bundling software in an existing popular Linux distribution, as exemplified by the wide availability of business partner programmes addressed to ISVs, is an excellent way to reduce marketing costs and increase public awareness of a product. One study indicates that the decision to release products under copyleft licences or to incorporate copyleft software in commercial products depends on a firm's existing intellectual property rights and patents portfolio and on hardware trademarks (Fosfuri et al., 2008). Firms with a reputation for delivering high-quality hardware may decide to release the software used to run their hardware under copyleft licences or to adopt an existing FL/OSS solution in order to reduce the costs of developing this software in-house and to avoid lock-in with software suppliers. The ability to exploit a patent portfolio can make firms more secure about releasing software under a copyleft licence. Sun Microsystems Inc. has surrounded its FL/OSS operating system, Solaris, with a range of patents (Fosfuri et al., 2008), although it grants FL/OSS developers the rights to use it.

The ability of FL/OSS to reach a diverse user and, especially, technical user base is an important motivation for releasing a mature proprietary application or platform under a copyleft licence. IBM's release of Eclipse is an example of a strategy aimed at establishing a positive feedback loop of adoption, development and use. In some cases, such a strategy is adopted to disrupt the spread of a competing technology. For example, the Netscape Corporation's decision to open source the Netscape Navigator browser led to the creation of the very successful FireFox browser and was a response, in part, to the dominance of Microsoft's Internet Explorer. However, the principal aim of this strategy is to attract contributions that will improve the software and goods that complement the technology which increase the value of the technology by putting it at the centre of a larger business eco-system (West, 2007). Nonetheless, as I show in the next section, the release of proprietary software under a copyleft licence does not imply handing over control to the FL/OSS community.

Research on the appropriability of scientific findings, on the reasons why firms choose to invest in scientific research despite the highly uncertain rate of return, and why they agree to publish results and make them available to rivals, offers important insights on the strategic use of FL/OSS in the business context (Rosenberg, 1989). First, the idea is contested that knowledge once produced is freely available to others (Hicks, 1995). This is because published papers often omit important information, such as the details of the methodology adopted or the experimental setup. Thus, they do not communicate the tacit knowledge often required to fully understand and replicate the research results.

The decision to adopt the FL/OSS route seems to depend not only on the firms' intellectually property rights portfolios, but also on the suitability of a FL/OSS strategy in relation to their core competencies and resources. The code that IBM donated to Eclipse, for example, was already compatible with its own tools and processes. Other companies wanting to use the Eclipse code were required to invest large amounts of time in order to be able to use it and to incorporate it efficiently into their own products. As is the case with the information presented in published scientific papers, availability of the source code does not make it simple to commoditize FL/OSS.

Next, akin to the benefits derived from basic scientific research, engagement in FL/OSS development sustains a variety of learning experiences that provide important advantages vis-à-vis competitors. In a 2007 paper titled 'Experiences on Product Development with Open Source Software', Nokia's head of open source strategy, Dr Ari Jaaksi, provides an interesting account of the challenges underlying the use of FL/OSS in Nokia's N770 and N800 Internet Tablets. The tablets run FL/OSS applications on top of an underlying layer, a platform that also consists of FL/OSS components and which can be used to develop additional programs and services.

In his article, Jaaksi describes how his team coped with FL/OSS developers' preferences for experimentation and lack of interest in delivering a stable product, by organizing the process of commercial development into two phases. In the first—experimentation—phase, the Nokia team worked closely with the community 'in true hacking mode' (Jaaksi, 2007: 92). In the second phase, the Nokia team discontinued its interactions with the FL/OSS community and focused on stabilizing the software by running tests and ironing out bugs—faults in the code. Another challenge for Jaaksi's team was related to the characteristic of FL/OSS projects as works in progress, where updated versions are released in rapid succession. The desire to remain current with the newest versions of FL/OSS (to benefit from incremental improvements and new features and avoid having to maintain existing versions of the software) is difficult to reconcile with the need to ensure backward compatibility, that is, to ensure that applications remain compatible over different product and platform generations. Ultimately, the team decided to address this dilemma by establishing stricter architecture management requirements and compatibility layers between the platform components and the applications.

Other benefits of engaging in FL/OSS development suggested in the literature on the way firms engage in scientific research include the ability to tap into important information networks. In the same way that scientists share information across organizational boundaries, participation in FL/OSS development appears to allow employees to keep updated with software developments and to exploit communities and networks of practice. However, engagement in FL/OSS development is born only out of a desire to capitalize on or extend the existing assets and capabilities of firms, or extract revenue from collectively produced public goods. In a videocast interview,[16] Jonathan Schwartz, Sun Microsystems' CEO, describes how the company is seeking to build broad developer communities as a way of promoting and sustaining innovation which will fuel demand for its products. Thus, for Sun Microsystems, developer communities are envisaged as both sources of innovation and the vehicles driving demand for its integrated systems.

DYNAMICS OF PARTICIPATION IN FIRM-INITIATED AND CONTROLLED FL/OSS PROJECTS

In the 2004 KDE Akademy conference in Ludwigsburg, Germany, the keynote speech was given by Erik Chambe-Eng, one of the founders of Trolltech ASA. He describes the relationship between his company and KDE as synergistic, founded upon KDE's role as a watershed for Trolltech ASA in driving sales of Qt, especially in Germany where many KDE developers are based; the company's policy of hiring KDE developers; KDE's role as a testbed for Qt in which each new version of the toolkit is thoroughly tested by a large group of volunteers; and KDE's showcasing of the Qt toolkit.

Chambe-Eng pointed out that the relationship between his firm and the community was consolidated with the creation of the KDE Free Qt Foundation which has ensured continuing access to the latest versions of Qt for the FL/OSS movement and KDE, in particular. Despite the long and fruitful relationship between the firm and the community, for a long time, KDE developers were not allowed access to its development tree. Many firms have attempted to reap the kinds of benefits of cooperation with FL/OSS communities described by Chambe-Eng by founding their own FL/OSS projects. This form of involvement entails extensive experimentation with different models and approaches to community building, and the organization of the development process. The reason for this experimentation is linked to the difficulties involved in finding a balance between a project evolution that serves the interests of the firm, external contributors' perceptions of what is fair and desirable in terms of decision making, and the ability to influence project development.

In the rest of this section I draw upon research on 'participation architecture' to compare the dynamics of sponsored, corporately initiated and controlled FL/OSS projects with those of community-initiated and -governed projects. This enables consideration of the effects of different legal, technical and participation arrangements on firms' abilities to mobilize and sustain volunteer contributions. In turn, this allows me to elaborate on the meaning of 'openness' and to specify the various levers and aspects of projects that firms retain control over or relinquish to communities.

Most successful grassroots-initiated FL/OSS projects develop gradually, both technically and socially. Their code base grows in line with the community of contributors. This facilitates learning by creating an evolving community of practice in which new contributors benefit from the experience of long-standing contributors and enables information generated by collective resources, such as project mailing lists, to be accessed. Firms that wish to attract volunteer contributions to their products are confronted by the challenge of introducing potential contributors to an existing and possibly complex code base (O'Mahony and West, 2005). In this case the nascent community is introduced to a complex system with no opportunity to develop a tacit understanding of the project architecture or of how the various components fit together and are supposed to work together (West and O'Mahony, 2005).

Research on modular technologies and their architectures indicates that one of the factors that may facilitate learning and the recruitment of external contributors is modularity (Baldwin and Clark, 2006). A system is regarded as modular when its parts can be designed independently, but they work together to support the whole. Compatibility between different parts, or modules, is achieved by architectural design rules. A modular structure allows contributors to make informed judgments about the pay-offs from their involvement in different parts of the code base by indicating, for example, whether it is better to contribute to an existing effort or to design a new module. Also, a modular design with a clearly defined architecture, in principle, allows contributors to focus on their chosen modules, without having to learn in detail about how all the elements of the system interact. Firms may try to alleviate the high start-up learning costs associated with the release of a mature code base by producing detailed project documentation and providing support through IRC channels and mailing lists.

Another important dimension of firm-initiated FL/OSS projects is the choice of licence and intellectual property rights control, that is, the question of who owns the copyright to the software. In order to ascertain their interests, some firms adopt their own product-specific or corporate licences, which impose different sets of restrictions on use, redistribution, commercialization and modification than the more widely used FL/OSS licences such as the GPL. This can introduce complexity by requiring developers to familiarize themselves with the specifics of a particular licence, and it can undermine volunteer participation by limiting what individual developers can do with the code (Shah, 2006). At the same time, there are indications that some developers may prefer licences with less restrictive terms than the GPL, such as the GNU Lesser General Public Licence (LGPL), but which do not extend the restrictions imposed by copyleft to other programs that connect with their product (Stewart et al., 2005). This is especially important for developers and companies that want to be able to use the software to develop proprietary applications. For example, after its acquisition by Nokia at the end of 2008, Trolltech ASA, by then called Qt Software, decided to adopt a tri-licensing scheme that makes Qt available through a GPL, a commercial licence and a LGPL. The choice of LGPL was to encourage firms to contribute any improvements they might make to Qt, providing an alternative to the all-or-nothing scenario under the earlier dual licensing scheme.

The ability to change licensing policy following the implementation of a new business model or the decision to expand the project's developer base are among the reasons why firms retain copyright ownership. When copyright is distributed among a large number of owners, a licence change becomes extremely complicated as each developer or organization that has ever contributed to the project needs to agree to the terms of the new licence.[17] In order to avoid such situations, many firms require external developers to hand over copyright on their contributions.

However, private ownership of code can also act as a disincentive to participation, as external developers may be disinclined to contribute to a project which, in principle, could restrict their future rights. Two important factors that weight external contributors' decisions to participate despite corporate ownership of copyright are the extent to which they need the software and the extent to which they trust the firm (Shah, 2006). In some cases, firms try to establish their legitimacy and reassure communities that code will remain available to their members by transferring ownership of the code base to a foundation created for this purpose.

Organization of the development process provides another set of parameters that firms may choose to achieve or relinquish control over the code. These include transparency of the production processes and accessibility of the development tree. In community-initiated and -managed FL/OSS projects, decisions about the directions of projects, the merits of different approaches and the implications of different choices are discussed—primarily on mailing lists. Public deliberation and debate are prerequisites for the establishment and maintenance of a collective sense of ownership and identity, but also are practical. They allow decentralized communities of globally distributed developers to keep abreast of the latest developments and to understand the reasoning behind certain choices. Both these factors are especially important for firms whose employees are the primary contributors to the development. Some FL/OSS start-up companies, such as Canonical Ltd, have made the conscious decision not to have central offices, thereby emulating the distributed process of FL/OSS development and requiring their employees to use the same communication tools and channels used by the rest of the community.

Access to the development tree involves several aspects. It includes the right to read and download the latest development snapshot, that is, the most recent functioning version of the program; the right to commit changes directly to the development tree; and the right to introduce bigger, more profound changes such as adding new modules. In this case, too, firms may experiment with different arrangements that confer different degrees of 'openness'. As pointed out earlier in this chapter, despite its close relationship with the KDE community, prior to 2009, Trolltech had no public access repository that allowed developers to check on the latest changes to the source code.

In community-managed FL/OSS projects, write access to the software repository and the ability to submit changes directly to the code base are important ways of regulating and establishing membership. Other forms of membership may involve participation in groups that help to manage different aspects of the development process and the project. Some communities have teams that help with the organization of the release process. Others, as in the case of GNOME and KDE, create non-profit foundations to represent them in legal and financial matters. Although some of these forms of membership are formalized through the codification of criteria outlining the conditions for inclusion, they are all dependent on an idea of authority that emerges from an established record of ability, contribution and involvement in community life.

Also, in community-managed FL/OSS projects, authority is distributed (Mateos-Garcia and Steinmueller, 2008). Typically, FL/OSS works without formal decision making, especially with regard to the technical evolution of a project, and decisions are made collectively through the processes of debate and negotiation. In order to ensure that projects evolve in a direction aligned to their chosen interests, firms may want to impose a more centralized form of governance. This may influence the degree of difficulty and the review process put in place for external contributions to be accepted to the development tree, authority over when new versions of the project are released, and the rules for membership in other groups and bodies and different levels of decision-making authority.

WHAT MAKES AN ETHICAL FL/OSS BUSINESS?

In this chapter a typology of firm engagement in FL/OSS has been established, and different forms of appropriation and the variety of strategies associated with them have been highlighted. I first outlined the various ways in which firms support and contribute to FL/OSS development, including monetary contributions, donations of software and hardware, patent pledges and release of proprietary software under copyleft licences. Examination of the business ecology of two grassroots-initiated and -managed FL/OSS communities highlights the different types of firms that commoditize FL/OSS projects. These include start-up insurgent firms, whose business depends largely on the provision of services and products around FL/OSS, and incumbents, or larger established corporations, which are intensive consumers and producers of FL/OSS. I discussed some of the most widely adopted revenue models associated with FL/OSS, such as service contracts and dual licensing.

My discussion of the strategic use of FL/OSS in the business context illustrates how its use depends on the firm's existing assets and capabilities and how participation in FL/OSS development can be viewed as a long-term strategy that supports the development of new skills, drives demand for complementary products and services, and promotes innovation. The consideration of corporately initiated and managed projects highlights some of the trade-offs between keeping a hold on the development reins and inviting and encouraging external contributions. If the reins are too tight, then external contributions cannot scale; if too loose, then the project might evolve in a direction that does not bring any value to the firm that initiated it.

It is clear that firms experiment continuously with different models and approaches; even successful strategies may be revised in view of changing market dynamics and opportunities. It is also clear that firms initiating FL/OSS projects are often keen to invite contributions from both individual contributors and also other firms. This suggests that we need to broaden our idea of what constitutes a 'contributor' or a 'volunteer' to take account of participation in FL/OSS as a specific aspect of company employment and policy. This is also interesting in the context of discussions about what constitutes an ethical FL/OSS business,[18] namely, what is the ideal partnership between firm and community? The key issue is the degree of transparency and openness in the processes of development and decision making and the nature of the firm's social responsibility in terms of what is given back to communities in acknowledgement of their contributions.

How should we understand these various expressions of firms as sponsors of, contributors to and initiators of FL/OSS projects? I have argued that it is difficult to attribute all the aspects of firm involvement to a single FL/OSS strategy. But, perhaps, if the different expressions of firm support and involvement in FL/OSS development are seen as part of the effort to maintain credibility in terms of the commitment to be a supportive and ethical participant in the FL/OSS community, then a strategic direction may be seen to exist.

The idea of 'credible commitment' comes from the tradition of institutional economics and was developed in order to address how different economic players are bound together by agreements that transcend space and time (North, 2008). According to Kenneth Shepsle (1991), quoted in North (2008), there are two types of credible commitment. The first relies on motivations and explains how actors create a framework of cooperation that is beneficial to everyone as long as its rules are followed. The gift economy can be understood as one such framework of cooperation. As we have seen, firms that initiate their own FL/OSS projects develop their own variations of the reciprocal FL/OSS development model. The second type of credible commitment, the imperative, takes effect when a player, in our case a firm involved in FL/OSS, relinquishes some of its power to impose its will on others. Patent pledges and transfers of control over copyright to the FL/OSS community can be regarded as expressions of this second type of credible commitment.

From this perspective, we can view the multiple aspects of firm involvement in FL/OSS as part of the effort to sustain credibility, trustworthiness and reputation as a 'good citizen' in the FL/OSS community. Credible commitments and the ability to uphold the positive social values associated with FL/OSS are crucial for ensuring that companies remain in a position to benefit from FL/OSS development in the long and the short term.

5 The Community, the Firm and the Two Economies

A study of software development by the Linux Foundation suggests that between 2005 and 2008, 70% of work on the Linux kernel was conducted by programmers employed by companies (Kroah-Hartman et al., 2008). In a book entitled *The Engineers and the Price System* Thomas Veblen (1921) conceives of scientists and engineers as a force engaged in efficient productive work and educated in the values of workmanship. He contrasts the emerging consciousness of engineers with the predatory nature of business people. In his view, business people profit by interrupting or hindering economic production because they devote more time to increasing product price than improving its utility.[1] Thus the fact that many contributors to the Linux kernel are employed by companies is likely to have disappointed Veblen greatly, but would have made Nicholas Carr successful in his wager with Yochai Benkler.

So, what does a study of the Linux kernel, the flagship of FL/OSS development, really reveal? Would Veblen have been disappointed, and would his disappointment have been justified? Are FL/OSS projects diminished by their becoming more and more integrated into the private sector? In this chapter I focus on the implications of commercialization for community-founded and -managed FL/OSS projects. Having examined how firms use FL/OSS to stimulate innovation, grow their businesses and develop their capabilities, I now consider how firms become engaged in *existing* community-founded and -managed FL/OSS projects.

In this context, firms do not have as great an ability to dictate the rules of the game as when they initiate their own FL/OSS projects and are required to find a balance between controlling the project and creating a framework of participation that will mobilize external contributors. In an existing community project, the firm wanting to join is the client, the co-developer or the guest in an established technical and social framework. I highlight the tensions and synergies that emerge from relations between the gift and the market economies from the perspective of volunteers, and emphasize the social character of the FL/OSS development process and the methods devised by firms and communities to negotiate and align their priorities and interests.

THE TWO VIEWS OF THE FIRM IN
GRASSROOTS FL/OSS DEVELOPMENT

How do firms engage in the framework of participation offered by grass-roots FL/OSS communities? I examine two distinct methods of firm engagement in volunteer-driven and community-managed FL/OSS projects. The first is the case where the firm participates as an *external* actor in an existing community and its development processes. In this case, the firm is the client or subcontractor. This type of corporate involvement is characterized by the absence of long-term ties with the community and involves a lack of willingness or ability on the part of the firm to engage fully in the community development process.

The second method involves firms acting as 'co-developers', cultivating sustained involvement in particular FL/OSS projects. This aspect of engagement involves the activities of insurgents or smaller firms, such as RedHat Inc., that specialize in developing products and services around FL/OSS, as well as incumbents or large firms, such as Nokia and IBM and Sun Microsystems Inc., whose involvement in FL/OSS is part of a broader business strategy. I refer to this as *embedded engagement*. It relies on the activities of employed contributors who, as in the case of Linux, play an active role in project development. As indicated in Chapter 2, the concept of embeddedness refers to the interpenetration of business and social relations. In this chapter I use the term to express the interpenetration of the professional and community ties of employed developers.

These two forms of engagement should be considered as distinct from the typology in Chapter 4 which refers to firms that initiate their own FL/OSS projects. The common denominator between firm initiators and firm clients, or co-developers, is the involvement of firm employees in the development process. The communities that are the focus of this chapter are independent of companies in terms of their initiation and governance and are the types of communities most commonly associated with the volunteer-based FL/OSS model of cooperation.

The evidence presented in this chapter includes the findings from my study of the GNOME and KDE projects, interviews conducted primarily with 23 contributors to the KDE and GNOME projects, and the results of my quantitative study of patterns of contribution and module ownership among volunteer and affiliated contributors from these communities. As has been shown, GNOME and the KDE are long-standing, mature and institutionally independent FL/OSS projects, whose technologies are used by a number of businesses (see Chapter 4).

FIRMS AS CLIENTS AND SUBCONTRACTORS

From the perspective of firms with little or no experience in FL/OSS, the FL/OSS development process can appear rather foreign compared to proprietary software production. Depending on the level of integration of FL/OSS in products and services there is a diverse set of issues that needs to be addressed. These include managing intellectual property rights and licensing issues—especially with regard to the implications of combining pieces of software that are protected by different licences. There is also a need to tailor FL/OSS to a company's needs and decisions about how to integrate it with existing systems. And there are other questions related to timing and quality control: if the release of new products and services is tied to new releases of FL/OSS, then it is crucial that these releases are regular and reliable.

After highlighting some general issues regarding the challenge of aligning community and commercial interests in the development process, I draw attention to the case of bounty hunts, which are a specific strategy for achieving control and improving alignment between firms and communities.

The FL/OSS project development cycle, including releases to the wider public of new improved versions of programs, may be feature or time based. In feature-based releases, the new, stable version is made available after improvements by developers; this is the approach adopted in the context of commercial development. However, there is a trend in mature FL/OSS towards time-based releases, meaning that succeeding versions are released on the basis of a specified, recurrent timeframe. Time-based releases, through their use of scheduling and their introduction of regularity in the release cycle, are evolving into important instruments for the organization and management of volunteer labour (Michlmayr, 2007). The regularized, time-based release cycles in FL/OSS projects are an important aspect of community-corporate alignment because they enable companies to time the release of their own products and make plans on the basis of future scheduled releases.

Some communities have made significant headway in aligning community and corporate processes and in addressing the needs of firms as clients. In 2001, GNOME adopted a six-month release cycle following prolonged discussion among community members about whether developers could comply with the more demanding rhythms of time-based releases. The GNOME Foundation manages the release cycle with input from a dedicated developer team.[2] At the end of 2008, KDE changed to a fixed time-based release schedule.

Generally, though, there are more gaps than areas of contact in terms of the integration of commercial requirements with community development processes. FL/OSS developers may be unwilling to work on specific features or to address faults that may be crucial for a company. Firms' and volunteers' priorities do not always coincide. Companies' QA processes are frequently incompatible with those of communities. Companies often have different ways of tracking faults in programs requiring different QA tests. Of course, there is nothing to prevent companies from developing the required features themselves, but their subsequent acceptance by the community is subject to certain requirements. A few projects have taken steps to alleviate some of the difficulties faced by firms with little experience in FL/OSS development. The Linux Foundation[3] has developed a non-disclosure agreement scheme to enable companies to hire external developers with experience in kernel development. This framework ensures that corporate contributions are properly reviewed, but that disclosure of firms' development plans is under their control.[4]

The following examples are based on individual interviews conducted in 2004–2005, with a sample of eight volunteer and fifteen firm-employed FL/OSS contributors, focusing on commercialization issues. Eleven of the interviews involved contributors from the GNOME and KDE projects and inquired about general issues related to alignment and control issues. Six interviews focused on the GNOME Bounty Hunt, a contest that awards cash prizes for solutions to specific problems and the development of new features. A further six focus on the challenges faced by the Gstreamer community in the early stages of its commercialization by Fluendo SL, the first company to use Gstreamer, which is a FL/OSS multimedia application, to create commercial products. The analysis also incorporates the results of a quantitative examination of GNOME and KDE networks of maintainers and members of the GNOME Foundation and KDE e.V. during the same period. My perspective of these cases was shaped by attendance at seven major community events.

My analysis of the interview materials indicates that company contributions are not always considered appropriate for projects. For example, the community may consider that a corporate contribution is too specialized in relation to the aims of the overall project and, consequently, 'pushes patches upstream', that is, that getting changes accepted by the code's original authors and integrated in the main development branch may be seen as irrelevant. Companies' objectives of pushing changes upstream are related to the savings in time and effort required to maintain the software in the long run. On the other hand, a corporate contribution may be very relevant. The ideal situation is for module maintainers to review proposed changes and, if found to be satisfactory, to adopt them. Maintainers may sometimes be reluctant to accept contributions, especially if they imply significant changes to the overall structure of the module.

In Chapter 4, I discussed how misalignment can occur through the inability of firms to follow rapid rates of project development. I showed how the Nokia team working on the development of its Internet Tablets was obliged to develop a strategy in order to balance the frequently faster rhythms of FL/OSS development with demands for integration, stability, interoperability and backward compatibility that characterize commercial systems and products incorporating FL/OSS. There is also a problem of balancing alignment and control from the perspective of programmers not familiar with the FL/OSS model of development. Twelve interviewees pointed out that programmers used to commercial development, when brought in to work on community projects, had to learn the ways of the community and adjust to the rhythms and the demands of FL/OSS development. One GNOME contributor described an early encounter between GNOME hackers and company employees:

> Oh, yes, I do remember one meeting with Sun in the early days, just an accidental one, cause some GNOME hackers were visiting Dublin and we went up to the big Sun headquarters there and we said, 'Release on time? No, we never release on time!' and the look of the people who were actually working for a living on it at Sun was that of absolute horror! 'What do you mean you don't release on time, we are relying on that date to ship to our customers!' (Sean,[5] 09.03.04)

One assumption underpinning the acceptance of code submitted by employed contributors is that it is on the same meritocratic basis as applies to the rest of the community. This is how a GNOME developer perceived this issue:

> If, in a project like GNOME people are very afraid, well not afraid, but aware of not letting the project like GNOME or KDE, or the Linux kernel or something like that be completely hijacked by commercial interests, like they, and I keep saying 'they', but I mean 'we' really, I am part of this, we are very happy to have commercial interests contributing resources by companies like Sun and Redhat and Novell and all of these big companies, like it is fantastic that they are devoting essentially hundreds of thousands of dollars of developer resources to help us out. But at the same time it has to be done on the same basis as when I contribute something to GNOME. It is, I am putting my code out there, it is open source, the community accepts it or rejects it, and there is no special favours given to someone just because they come from a company with a big name and sort of millions of dollars in revenue each year. (Al, 24.06.04)

The case of Wipro Ltd is illustrative of some of these issues. Wipro Ltd is an Indian software house which in 2002 was subcontracted by Sun Microsystems Inc. to help develop GNOME 2.0, the desktop and applications development environments for the Solaris operating system, which is Sun's version of Unix. Although Wipro developers were expected to contribute to development, their contributions were not envisaged as long term. Their success was gauged according to specific metrics (bugs fixed, bugs logged), and they were not expected to participate in the social aspects of the project. Due to the lack of prior knowledge about the GNOME code base and the lack of relevant documentation, they were obliged to resort to GNOME community mailing lists and IRC channels to obtain information. The presence of a dozen developers all asking questions and requiring answers strained the learning resources of the community and created a stir among developers. The situation was further complicated by the fact that Wipro's contribution was not visible to, and hence was not understood by, the community. Martin, a GNOME developer, who at the time was working for Sun Microsystems Inc., observed:

> So they were on IRC asking us very intelligent questions but you would see very little end result for the questions, you know what I mean? So that kind of thing is invisible, it is impossible to see what they are actually doing, or how they are actually achieving anything. Now, behind the scenes I know exactly what they are doing, what they were doing, they have been working very, very hard for Sun, but in terms of being visible, kind of within the community? (Martin, 11.07.04)

Bounties—cash prizes for solving specific problems or implementing certain features—are an alternate form of subcontracting that some companies use to influence the development process. The case of the GNOME Bounty Hunt contest illustrates some of the challenges associated with such methods and their potential for satisfying user needs. The GNOME Bounty Hunt was initiated by Novell Inc. at the end of 2003. It had two phases over a period of approximately 18 months. The contest comprised 45 prizes or bounties ranging from US$ 15 to US$ 2,500, the most frequent being $US 500. Overall, Novell planned to spend US$ 24,315. Many of these bounties related to the integration of data across different personal information management applications, such as calendar, mail client and address book, and a substantial number relating to Evolution, the personal and group information management program developed by the company.

According to Novell's Vice President, Nat Friedman, one of the founders of GNOME and the person who had come up with the idea of the contest, the bounties had three aims: to motivate people to think about the integration of personal information on the desktop; to bring in new developers to GNOME; and to urge the community to start thinking about bounties as a sustainable form of interaction with external actors. The rules of the contest stated that for a bounty to be claimed, the work had to be accepted by the relevant module maintainer and become part of the subsequent GNOME release.

Problems soon began to emerge. Although mailing list postings reflected general agreement that, as the sponsor, Novell had the right to specify the bounties, there was some objection to the technical choices they emphasized. Some were seen as undermining the authority of maintainers to specify the directions of their modules and the previously agreed upon project policies. This applied both to certain high-level choices, such as the decision to implement particular features in FireFox rather than in Epiphany, GNOME's default Internet browser, and to specifically requested features which some maintainers did not deem suitable for their modules. The contest added to the maintainers' workloads because of the requirement that, for solutions to be eligible for an award, they needed to be accepted by maintainers and integrated in the subsequent release. Some argued that the bounties associated with Evolution were meant to kick-start participation in the project, whose rapid rate of development created an important barrier to entry for volunteers.

Putting aside the challenges brought by the organization and implementation of the contest, it is worth considering it as a way to address the needs of external actors. In an extensive blog entry,[6] Nat Friedman elaborated his idea to introduce a general bounty system that would allow anyone working on FL/OSS to specify and claim a bounty. In his view, it provided users with an opportunity to get closer to developers. Friedman had conceived of a system where both organizations and individuals could bid collectively in order to improve certain aspects of programs. One interviewee suggested that bounties might be a way of putting pressure on maintainers to implement features that they would not normally have contemplated. In this context, consider the following post on GNOME bounties from a GNOME developer who runs a small software business:

Hi all,
What ever happened to gnome bounties? I've only followed this list for a year, but I see from the archives that there have been a variety of controversies about them—but nothing really definitive.

I think it would be useful to do some like: 1) Allow someone trusted (with commit access? foundation member? bug editor?) to flag a bug in bugzilla as so-annoying-I'll-pay-to-have-it-fixed (gnome-money vs gnome-love?). 2) Let a module maintainer vet the offer (to reject unwanted features or things that will be fixed soon anyway). 3) Have a list of active bounties. 4) Maybe pay through the Foundation (not sure about that). Right now, we have big companies that can devote developers (Novell, Red Hat) or run formal bounty-esque programs (Google SOC), but nothing that can really tap the concerns of smaller organizations or individuals. As an example, I use Gnome in my small company, and I've submitted plenty of small patches. But my skills are limited, and I can't devote that much time to fixing bigger things. But I could pay a few hundred dollars... bug 388152 is an example of something I'd pay for (make evince scale printed pages in a natural way). Did the foundation come out against bounties on principle, or has the idea just not gone anywhere?

From: 'Dr. Michael J. Chudobiak' <mjc avtechpulse com>
To: foundation-list gnome org
Subject: bounties? Date: Tue, 06 Nov 2007 09:48:13 -0500

In the context of community-driven projects, bounties raise some important questions about how requests are expressed, prioritized and implemented. These issues touch on the balance of power between contestants, maintainers, the individuals controlling project development within the community, and external actors—whether individual users, firms or public institutions.

Contests such as this are usually more controversial than other forms of subcontracting because they are more visible. They highlight more forcefully the issue of monetary incentives and the balance between the gift and market economies.

An additional dimension to bounties involves the design and implementation of a broad technical intervention. This goes against the established idea of an emergent FL/OSS development agenda, which is shaped by the accumulated decisions of the technical leaders in the community. Another example of coordinated intervention is the GNOME outreach project,[7] an initiative promoted by the GNOME Foundation to sponsor tasks related to improving accessibility in GNOME. The contest is sponsored by the GNOME Foundation, Novell Inc., Canonical Ltd, Google and the Mozilla Foundation.

A key issue in these types of initiatives is the engagement of community members in the formulation and the implementation of the development agenda incorporated in the specified prizes. Novell Inc.'s failure to do this was one of the reasons why the GNOME Bounty Hunt was controversial, which brings us back to the question of how requests originating from actors external to the community can be fulfilled and how such systems can be designed.

THE EMBEDDED VIEW OF THE FIRM

Firms that develop products and services based on FL/OSS may be aiming at sustained involvement in community-driven projects through co-development. This embedded form of firm involvement relies on the contributions of employed contributors with close FL/OSS community ties. The research on which this chapter is based indicates that these employees may be programmers who gradually develop an understanding of the FL/OSS development process as part of their employment or programmers who previously worked as volunteers. All but one of the 15 employed developers working in the GNOME, KDE and Gstreamer projects who were interviewed had previously been volunteers.

There are significant advantages in hiring FL/OSS developers with experience in the projects that companies seek to commercialize. First, they are familiar with the technical aspects of the projects—with the source code and the specifications of the project architecture. Second, they are familiar with the social processes of FL/OSS development. They understand the norms and values and the negotiation processes that underlie the technical evolution of projects. Third, they have had the opportunity to develop networks of connections which they can exploit in order to mobilize support around a change they wish to make or seek help to solve a particular problem. This form of engagement involves a more subtle form of control than that implied by firm participation as an external actor in the development process. This is because employed contributors arguably are better placed, due to their expertise and social standing, to serve firm interests than is achievable through any formalized process or alignment technique.

In order to understand the effects of employment relations on community activities, I examine them in the context of two overlapping, but distinctive, groups: (i) members of the GNOME Foundation and KDE e.V., and (ii) the GNOME and KDE's maintainer networks. The data on GNOME Foundation and KDE e.V. members were gathered mainly through an email survey conducted in 2006 which yielded 199 responses from GNOME Foundation members (59.4% response rate) and 63 responses from KDE e.V. members (55.7% response rate). The data on maintainers' networks refer to maintainers involved in GNOME's 2.10 and KDE's 3.4 versions, both of which were released in March 2005. For GNOME, the analysis includes 110 modules maintained by 92 individuals; for KDE it includes 191 modules owned by 111 developers.

To recap, the GNOME Foundation and KDE e.V. are non-profit organizations that support the aims of the two projects and provide assistance in legal and financial matters. Membership is formalized, and applicants must demonstrate that they have made significant contributions to their respective community's project. These can include non-coding contributions such as translations and documentation. Applications for membership need to be endorsed by existing community members. Maintainership or module ownership is granted, usually informally, on the basis of technical excellence and commitment to the project. Maintainers are among the most highly regarded members of the community and have a major say in the development process. The term 'volunteer' is used here to refer to developers who indicated that they were not sponsored to contribute.

Analysis of the data obtained from GNOME Foundation members indicates an almost even split between employed and volunteer contributors. Of the 199 respondents, 98 were volunteers and 101 were employed. Employed developers belonged to one of three categories: employed to work exclusively on GNOME (38); employed to work on GNOME and other FL/OSS projects (35); and employed to work on FL/OSS, but not GNOME (28). As indicated in Chapter 4, developers were sponsored by a variety of organizations including large corporations, small and medium enterprises (SMEs) and research institutions. The three most important employers were Red Hat Inc. and Novell Inc. with 12 developers each, and Sun Microsystems Inc. with 16 developers.

Volunteers and employed members were also fairly evenly split in KDE e.V. with 34 out of 63 respondents indicating that they were volunteers, 19 had been employed to work exclusively on KDE, 5 had been employed to work on KDE and other FL/OSS projects and 5 had been hired to work on FL/OSS projects other than the KDE. As indicated in Chapter 4, the most important employers were Novell Inc. with five employees and Trolltech ASA Klarälvdalens Datakonsult AB with three employees each.

There were some differences in the patterns of contributions between volunteer and employed members depicted in Figure 5.1, which shows the volunteer GNOME foundation and KDE e.V. members in four areas of development,[8] indicating how effort is distributed within each group.

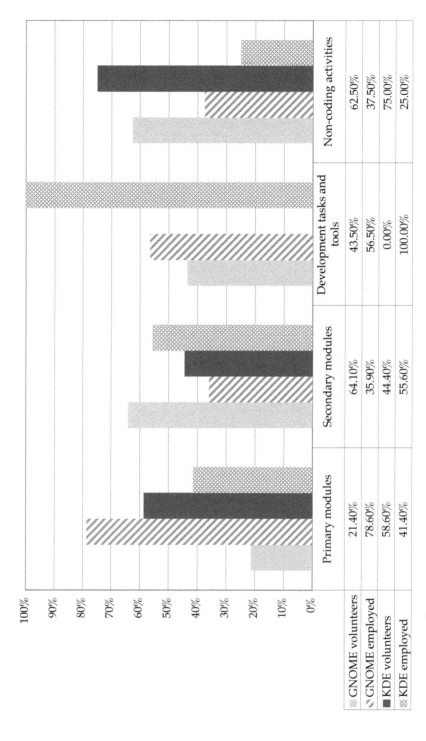

Figure 5.1 Distribution of effort by group according to reported main area of development. (Source: GNOME Foundation survey, N=199, KDE e.V. survey, N=63)

	Primary modules	Secondary modules	Development tasks and tools	Non-coding activities
GNOME volunteers	21.40%	64.10%	43.50%	62.50%
GNOME employed	78.60%	35.90%	56.50%	37.50%
KDE volunteers	58.60%	44.40%	0.00%	75.00%
KDE employed	41.40%	55.60%	100.00%	25.00%

In order to understand the distinction between primary and secondary modules, we need some more detail on the architectures of the two projects. As pointed out in Chapter 4, GNOME and KDE are multi-level projects that appeal to both the developer and the end-user communities. They provide a complex GUI environment, a suite of end-user applications and a collection of underlying programming libraries and components required to develop the GUI and the applications that exploit it. Primary modules include the main underlying programming and graphical libraries, the building blocks of the desktop and the platform. Changes in these areas are critical to the success of the project and can affect the entire development process. Secondary modules include end-user applications included in the respective distributions and some of the secondary parts of the GUI and the development platform which are important from the point of view of architectural design. Development tasks include activities, such as bug triaging[9] and release management, that are essential for quality control, integration and porting. Non-coding activities include aspects of software development such as translation, documentation, web maintenance and conference organization that support project dissemination, learning and collaboration more generally.

In the case of KDE e.V., there appear to be differences between paid and volunteer efforts in some areas of development. Volunteer activity is conspicuously absent in development tasks and tools (0%), whereas the rate of volunteer participation in non-coding activities (75%) is triple the participation of employed developers. The GNOME sample is larger, and the differences between the two groups are more pronounced. Infrastructure primary modules are mostly developed by hired contributors (78.6%) with peripheral tasks carried out predominantly by volunteers (62.5%). More detailed analysis of the data reveals that in the case of GNOME these patterns are statistically significant (χ^2 (df=3, N=199)= 27.2, p.<.001). Statistical significance indicates that the observed connections between employment or not and the area of development cannot be attributed to chance. Therefore, at least in the case of GNOME, paid developers and volunteer contributors would seem to have distinct profiles in terms of their main areas of contribution. Unsurprising, perhaps, is that the associations between contribution and employment are stronger in the case of developers hired to work exclusively or partly on GNOME.

The patterns of attendance of the two groups in the annual conferences of the two communities allow us to assess GNOME Foundation and KDE e.V. volunteers' and affiliated members' frequency of participation in these major events. I asked survey respondents to report their attendance over three years (2003–2006). The GNOME event is GUADEC, and the KDE annual conference is Akademy. These are important social and work-related events. They allow community members to renew existing and forge new collaborative ties; they offer opportunities to exchange ideas and facilitate coordination by encouraging

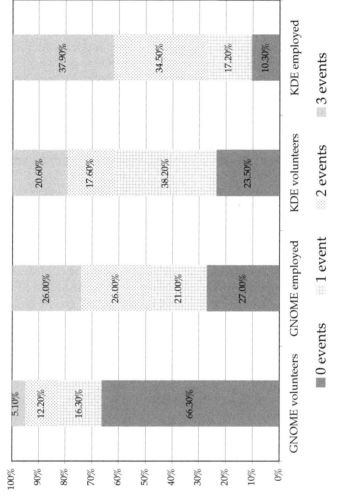

Figure 5.2   Event attendance. (Source: GNOME Foundation survey, N=199, KDE e.V. survey, N=63 [respondents])

people to agree on priorities and deadlines, which usually results in a flurry of development activity. Contrary to the widely accepted view of FL/OSS development, FL/OSS developers meet frequently. The terrain of FL/OSS related community events—which vary in terms of attendance, scope and recurrence—has not been mapped, but such events are vital for community coherence and development.

Figure 5.2 shows that employed developers in both groups attend community conferences more regularly than volunteers. Seven out of ten KDE affiliated developers attended a minimum of two events, whereas only four out of ten KDE volunteers had a similar record of attendance. At the same time, more than half of GNOME volunteers did not participate in any community events. More detailed analysis reveals that project-specific employment is the deciding factor in high attendance rates. In other words, more regular community event participants are more likely to meet developers hired to work on GNOME than volunteers. Given the costs of travel and accommodation that participation entails, this pattern of participation is not surprising (although both projects often cover the expenses of some volunteers). These events provide an important context for progressing work in that they allow developers to collaborate face to face in order to address difficult problems and to make plans for the future.

The patterns of activity of volunteers and sponsored contributors can be seen through an examination of module 'ownership'. Maintainers, the primary owners of the project modules, play a key part in the release of new versions in ensuring that the code for which they are responsible is ready on time and works smoothly with the other project components. They also act as gatekeepers who, over the course of the development cycle, control and review what is being integrated in 'their' modules. More importantly, perhaps, they formulate a vision of development for their areas of responsibility, dictate priorities and contribute collectively to the emergence of a technical agenda. Their responsibilities are based on their technical abilities and commitment, and they sit at the top of a project's meritocracy, which underlies the social organization of FL/OSS.

The results presented next were obtained by analysing online data pertaining to the GNOME 2.10 and KDE 3.4 versions, released in March 2005.[10] The network of GNOME maintainers consists of 92 individuals, split fairly evenly between 42 non-sponsored and 50 sponsored individuals. The majority of modules (76.4%) were maintained by one person; a significant number (21%) was managed by two developers; and a small number of critical, primary modules (4.5%) was maintained by teams of three or four developers. The ratio of paid to volunteer developers is lower in the case of KDE, with 72 volunteers and 39 sponsored developers. The proportion of modules maintained by a single individual is higher in KDE at 84.8%. Instances of modules being owned cooperatively by sponsored and volunteer developers were few for both projects: only 3% in KDE and 6% in the case of GNOME.

In both projects, sponsored developers maintain those parts of the code base where ownership appears to matter the most in terms of overall project impact, that is, at the level of infrastructural software components. Figure 5.3 illustrates differences in the patterns of (exclusive) maintainership between sponsored and volunteer developers (it excludes the few cases where maintainership is shared between volunteers and employed programmers). In GNOME employed developers maintained 78% of primary modules, in KDE 62.7%. These results are statistically significant. For GNOME χ^2 (df=3, N=103 modules)= 11.93, p.<.05 and for KDE χ^2 (df=2, N=176 modules)=25.76, p.<.05. This implies a level of trust in the ability of sponsored developers to make decisions that could affect the entire project, and such trust can only be built over time. Individual sponsored developers also consistently maintain more modules than volunteers. One in three (30.8%) sponsored KDE developers maintained more than two modules, but only one in six (15.3%) volunteers maintained more than two modules. In GNOME a sponsored developer is 4.5 times more likely than a volunteer to maintain more than two modules.

Although these results illustrate very clearly the importance of employment relations in volunteer projects, they do not capture the complexity of the dependencies that develop among communities, firms and employees. Employed developers, for example, often maintain modules that they are not directly paid to contribute to. That firms can dictate the agenda and the direction of projects because they hire key contributors is true only to the extent that these contributors' actions are determined by the directions that they receive from their employers and the coincidence between their own motivations and the objectives of their employers.

In order to have a better understanding of the embedded view of the firm introduced at the beginning of this chapter, it is necessary to examine the role of paid developers, the factors that shape their experience of collaboration and employment, and how they perceive and try to balance community and corporate interests. Developers with extensive cooperative and social ties carry with them a network of connections and a depth of know-how of community processes that facilitates their work in terms of its acceptance by the community, and provides a connection between corporate and community teams. In companies such as Sun Microsystems Inc., which have large teams of developers working on FL/OSS projects, these individuals often act as boundary spanners or intermediaries between the rest of the corporate team and the community. From the point of view of community, their long-term involvement and demonstrated technical skills endow them with a legitimacy that is not easily challenged.

At the same time, employed developers with a strong sense of community identity will demonstrate considerable sensitivity to community issues, which makes them cautious about attempting to balance community and company interests. Although some paid developers admitted that, on occasion, managing community-company boundaries was challenging, many interviewees

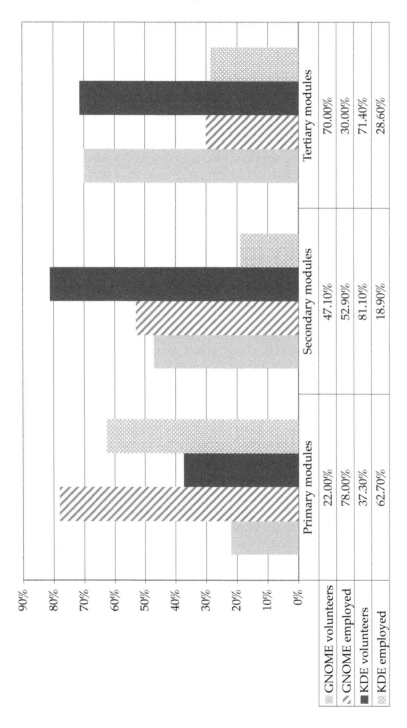

	Primary modules	Secondary modules	Tertiary modules
GNOME volunteers	22.00%	47.10%	70.00%
GNOME employed	78.00%	52.90%	30.00%
KDE volunteers	37.30%	81.10%	71.40%
KDE employed	62.70%	18.90%	28.60%

Figure 5.3   Maintainership. (Source: Online search, GNOME N=103, KDE N=176 [modules])

did not think that the roles of paid developer and community member were inherently incompatible. Several suggested in fact that their work did not necessarily conflict with a community identity. When asked how he managed the interests of firm and community, one interviewee observed:

> It was easy in Sun, because I was the only one doing that. So if I dropped something that was something: if I basically tried to get out of going something that was important to Sun but that was not important to GNOME, there would always be someone else to do it. I wouldn't have to make a big deal out of that. I would just subtly kind of put it on the side and somebody else would have to pick it up. I was doing enough good stuff anyway, so I could drop these other things on the side, so it never really became an issue. But if it had become an issue, when, say, my manager wanted me to work on some project for four months that was proprietary and, you know, it was no good to the free software community and stuff like that and that could have happened, it never did, but it could have happened, I would have be considering my position in Sun basically, you know, I would be considering leaving, if that happened like that. (Leroy, 18.3.04)

An important factor affecting these developers' relations with their employers and their everyday working lives is their companies' links with the projects and the FL/OSS communities in general. In the case of companies[11] with strong ties with the FL/OSS world, the confluence between community and corporate interests appears fairly straightforward. The fact that management understands community processes and policies makes relationships easier. More importantly, the act of upholding community values and ideals seems to be able to be conducted not in opposition (we and the rest of the company), but collectively (we in FL/OSS).

However, the ability of employees who previously worked as volunteers to manage community and corporate agendas such that they are detrimental to neither party is less certain. Even assuming that there are no real objections to the strategy or to the implications of a short- or long-term strong, hands-on presence in a FL/OSS project, it may be difficult to manage conflicting agendas. At the same time, we cannot assume that the confluence between community and corporate interests will be without its problems in the case of companies with a developed FL/OSS culture.

For example, I witnessed a discussion between Dan, an employed GNOME developer working for a GNOME spin-off company, and Jim, a FL/OSS developer recently hired by a company. Dan referred to the case of some developers who had started a company that was created as a spin-off from a FL/OSS project 'who were thinking community, community, community and then one day they woke up and they realized, that, shit! I am corporate'. According to Dan, the earlier these lines are drawn, the less trouble Jim's people would encounter in negotiating their double identities.

'What are you going to do', asked Dan, 'if your clients push you to deliver a product?'

Some of the complexity in the blurring of boundaries is illustrated by the case of Gstreamer and Fluendo SL. The Fluendo SL company, which is based in Barcelona, was founded in 2004 and utilizes Gstreamer to develop proprietary products and services such as Flumotion—a media-streaming server. At the time of my study in 2005, most of the company's employed developers had worked on Gstreamer as volunteers. Having been volunteers previously, these Fluendo SL programmers were sensitive to the fact that any acceleration in the company's rate of development would need to be gradual to give the community time to adjust. The faster rate of the company branch was increasing the amount of knowledge required, by increasing the number of changes that needed to be understood by the volunteer community. The volunteer community was contributing on a part-time basis, and the increased number of changes was accelerating the rate of learning needed for the community to make a substantive contribution before the next release.[12] The Fluendo SL developers, however, found it difficult to balance their efforts to make the community understand the need for a faster pace of development with keeping the development process transparent by replicating their group discussions online.

The Fluendo employees interviewed for my study thought that Fluendo SL's goals for Gstreamer coincided with what, at the time, they perceived to be the community's goals for the project. However, there was concern that this might not always be the case. Support for digital rights management and online sale of proprietary codecs were two choices that Fluendo employees expected would be controversial within the broader FL/OSS community. The company was attempting to overcome potential problems through its support of the Xinth Foundation, a non-profit organization that promotes open media formats. However, in 2007 many of the company's key employees resigned and were hired by another firm developing products and services on top of Gstreamer.

This highlights the problem of whether and how different firm interests can be served within the context of the same project. One contributor suggested that bodies such as the GNOME Foundation afford the opportunity for companies involved in projects to keep abreast of each other's activities and avoid nullifying each other's efforts. In terms of recruitment practices, several interviewees believed that companies prefer to hire volunteers who are already on a critical path in the project, who are heavily involved in central aspects of development and who have demonstrated that they are highly competent technically. In order to decide which Debian contributors to hire, for example, Mark Shuttleworth allegedly scanned six months' worth of Debian mailing list archives.[13]

This occurs at other levels than the individual: there are numerous examples of corporations buying into FL/OSS human capital through vertical integration. Novell Inc. achieved it through Ximian, a firm created by two of the GNOME project founders, and SUSE, a company selling a Linux distribution that used KDE. Both projects include Novell developers. In 2008 Nokia acquired Trolltech, which develops the programming libraries that form the building blocks of KDE, and Sun Microsystems recently bought MySQL, the company behind the development of one of the most popular FL/OSS databases.

These examples of community-integrated employees suggest that the issue of community-corporate relations is more complex than if the company is viewed as an external actor in a development process, whose influence is mediated by appropriately developed institutional interfaces. The grounding of professional relations in social relations can reinforce an individual's position in the hierarchy. The ability to work on projects on a full-time basis provides more opportunities for affiliated developers to ascend the meritocratic order than volunteers, who often can only work on projects in their spare time.

COMMUNITY, THE GIFT AND MARKET ECONOMIES

Veblen framed the emerging class consciousness of the workforce in terms of a sense of professional identity and a contrasting business rationality. The prevalent thinking about FL/OSS is rather different. FL/OSS communities have often been considered to occupy a space between the organized supply of markets and services occupied by firms, and the wider, emergent dynamics of software supply and demand. The boundaries to this space are often considered to be clearly demarcated and defined on the basis of seemingly antithetical pairs of ideas. On the one hand, there is the logic of the market economy in which people are driven by the desire for profit, transactions can be mapped by visible flows of money and capital and resources are scarce. On the other hand, there is FL/OSS, which is seen as operating in the domain of the gift economy, in which individuals are driven by enlightened self-interest and the desire to contribute to the creation of a common good from which they themselves benefit. In this context, system coordination is said to be achieved through a common set of values— the gift culture, a shared sense of community and a legal framework that formalizes reciprocity. It comprises abundance, reflected in the number of contributions that create an outcome that is greater than the sum of its parts. There are variations of this dichotomous thinking about FL/OSS, with some propositions more elaborate and convincing than others.

However, a rather different picture emerges from experience and systematic empirical investigation. Commercially driven open source projects form only one set of the possibilities created through the intersection of the gift and market economies. An alternative, described in this chapter, concerns the commercialization of communities that are independent from companies in terms of initiation and governance.

In the wider FL/OSS community the gift and market economies are not regarded as oppositional. Firm involvement can be regarded as a sign of project maturity and as an indication of resources being brought into the project that could potentially attract more volunteers (Stewart et al., 2005). Community and commercial motivations, however, persistently are conceptualized as divergent. Veblen's idea of the contrasting rationalities between businessmen and engineers re-emerges as a question of fundamental motives: FL/OSS developers strive for technical excellence and ethics; businesses want to make money. There are two problems with this conceptualization. The first concerns the audience, the FL/OSS user base, which no longer is restricted to the technical community of programmers and system administrators, but is reaching out to a more general set of end users and is leading to an increasing number of spin-off and other related initiatives, whose success depends upon the community. As a consequence, usability and localization, for example, are becoming increasingly important. And although the continuing priority for business is to make money, there are various ways to achieve it, especially in terms of relationships with volunteers.

In the course of the analysis in this chapter, I have highlighted some of the expectations of FL/OSS developers from company involvement in volunteer projects. Based on my analysis of the interview data these include a degree of transparency with regard to their agendas, compliance with licensing terms and acceptance of volunteer and employee contributions on the same grounds. These are not straightforward requirements, but form part of a broader discussion about what constitutes an ethical FL/OSS business, a discussion that has been stifled somewhat by an overemphasis on FL/OSS business models (Behlendorf, 1999; Krishnamurthy, 2005; West, 2003). This emphasis reflects a justifiable interest in the commercial appropriation of the work of FL/OSS communities, but provides only one vantage point from which to investigate the relationship between the gift and market economies.

Furthermore, a sharp distinction between businesses and engineers is not convincing in light of the considerable number of FL/OSS developers who make a living from FL/OSS—as occasional subcontractors, full-time employees or business people. The role of employed developers in FL/OSS development is receiving increased attention in the literature (Dahlander and Wallin, 2006; Henkel, 2008; Lin, 2006; Shah, 2006), and initial evidence on the different types of financial benefits from participation in FL/OSS is provided by some early, large-scale surveys of FL/OSS contributors (David et al., 2003).

Corporate presence does not necessarily undermine the volunteer basis of projects. Indeed, companies and communities may have similar interests in maintaining the balance in favour of the gift economy. Whether or not the presence of companies is viewed positively by volunteers is another issue, however. Stewart, Ammeter and Maruping (2005) indicate that users consider sponsorship to be an indication of a project's quality and reliability.

Lerner and Tirole (2002), on the other hand, argue that commercialization may be undesirable from the point of view of developers because it can render their contributions less visible to the wider FL/OSS community and limit their ability to tailor the software to their needs.

An evaluation of firm involvement in FL/OSS communities needs to go beyond examination of the formal, institutional and legal requirements and must take account of which areas affiliated developers contribute to, their role in development and their community ties. As we have seen, affiliated developers have a strong presence in GNOME's and KDE's leading non-profit organizations: they maintain critical parts of the code base, have an important say in the formulation of the development agenda and are regular attenders at community events.

For some researchers and advocates of FL/OSS, the crux of the relationship between the gift and exchange economies lies in the balancing of intrinsic and extrinsic incentives (Bonaccorsi and Rossi, 2006; Haruvy et al., 2003; Shah, 2006). Intrinsic motivations have been associated with activities that satisfy basic psychological needs such as enjoyment, competence and control. In the case of FL/OSS developers, intrinsic motivations are said to include the pleasure derived from problem solving and learning and the satisfaction gained from contributing to a public good (Lakhani and Wolf, 2005). The underlying assumption, which has it roots in Frey and Jegen's (2001) crowding-out theory, is that there is a point after which extrinsic motivations can overturn, or crowd out, intrinsic motivations.

There are two problems with understanding the relation between the gift and market economies as a balance between oppositional sets of motivations. First, the models of human behaviour implied by an opposition between intrinsic and extrinsic motivation are quite simplistic. Individuals can be motivated by extrinsic and intrinsic motivations simultaneously. FL/OSS contributors can drop in and out of employment while continuing to work on projects. The weaknesses of these approaches have been acknowledged and are being addressed through the elaboration of more complex models (Krishnamurthy, 2006; Roberts et al., 2006). The relationship between the gift and market economies cannot be reduced entirely to a question of motivations because this would not take full account of the social and collaborative contexts in which individuals operate. The analysis in this chapter indicates that employed developers with close community ties are sensitive to the needs and interests of the communities in which they participate. Their commitment is recognized by volunteers, who may elect them to high positions. However, communities are not blind to potential dangers. For example, the regulations of the GNOME Foundation limit the number of affiliated developers on its Board of Directors, the body that runs the foundation, which protects against any moves that might lead to a capture of the community. Moreover, the mandates that sponsored developers receive from their employers influence, but do not wholly determine, the direction of their work on a project.[14]

The overlaying of professional employment relations with social relations, the embeddedness of FL/OSS development and the meritocratic basis of participation can limit corporate influence in peer-established and institutionally independent projects. These characteristics of FL/OSS development create two additional challenges for FL/OSS projects. The first is how they respond to user needs and requirements. In the context of FL/OSS development, it is often unclear how user requirements can be addressed, when users—be they companies, individuals or the public—lack the skills, time or willingness to participate in the development process. Users are often expected to express their needs by submitting requests to the bug-management system. However, this assumes a degree of technical competency (at the very least knowledge about what is expected of them and how to express and submit such requests). Bounties represent one way to deal with this issue, but there is no prize or bid system in operation that can satisfy this need comprehensively.

The second challenge is the degree of control that institutionally independent FL/OSS projects have over their development agendas, project priorities and adoption of standards. The received wisdom is that FL/OSS development evolves organically, without centralized control, or through public deliberation over major decisions. However, this hands-off approach can lead to de facto decisions being made by whoever is in a position to effect major change, which includes firms employing core FL/OSS developers. Should communities deliberate over certain issues, and, if so, what regulatory mechanisms would be appropriate? Some of the issues here, such as how user requirements might be taken into account, are not strictly associated with the commercialization of FL/OSS. They concern the broader issues of growth and sustainability, and of reaching out to a broader audience of users and contributors, which are the focus of Chapter 6.

6 Learning and the Division of Labour in FL/OSS

Is FL/OSS development only about programming? Is programming only about programming? The heavily technological, software-production orientation of FL/OSS projects would seem to render such questions redundant. Yet, when browsing some of the project websites, even those hosted on large source code repositories, it is clear that there are many other dimensions to FL/OSS development. One of the most obvious is the people who maintain these websites and manage the infrastructure for software development. For example, who manages the VCS accounts and updates websites? Who responds to queries and maintains the Help/Frequently Asked Questions (FAQ) sections? The complexity of the tasks involved increases with the size of the project, making them more distinctive, and the roles easier to identify.

Many large projects organize annual community events that often involve hundreds of developers. In some cases, individuals are assigned explicitly to coordinating releases of new versions. In others, responsibility for advocacy, legal and funding activities is assigned to non-profit organizations or consortia involving community and corporate stakeholders. The GNOME and Apache Foundations and the Linux consortium are examples of FL/OSS organizations operating within recognizable legal frameworks. Depending on their user base, FL/OSS communities provide sets of learning materials and mobilize wide ranges of skill sets and types of expertise. The GNOME and KDE projects have dedicated teams of translators, documenters, usability and accessibility experts, and artists. These non-coding aspects of FL/OSS development, which complement code development and which are associated with improvements to users' overall experience, are discussed here and described as 'autonomous peripherality'.

Learning and mobilization of labour are at the heart of the growth and sustainability of FL/OSS communities. The high attrition rates and the inconsistency of contributions mean that without the influx of new developers, projects would wither and die. Also, as developer bases become larger, the need for individuals with broader skill sets increases: for example, GNOME and KDE are translated into more than 50 languages. So, what are the specific challenges involved in integrating new contributors, and how do we understand non-coding contributions in the context of such technologically intensive projects? To answer the first part of the question we need to develop an understanding of the learning challenges involved in becoming a productive contributor. To answer the second part, it is necessary to broaden our conceptualization of the development process and understand the connections and gaps between the work of programmers and non-programmers.

This chapter draws empirical evidence from 21 in-depth interviews with participants in GNOME and KDE projects, focusing on the subjects of learning and autonomous peripheral participation. It also draws on the results of my survey of the GNOME Foundation and KDE e.V. members in order to examine the relationship between employment and autonomous peripherality.

LEARNING IN FL/OSS: REVISITING QUESTIONS OF EXCELLENCE AND ACCESS

> There is a certain kind of make up that it takes to become an open source developer and I think that the process of becoming one can of to a certain extent ensure that that's true. (Sam, 14.04.04)

Learning is often considered a primary motive for participating in FL/OSS development (David et al., 2003; Ghosh et al., 2002; Lakhani and Wolf, 2005). The achievement of high levels of technical proficiency is at the heart of the hacker culture, where pleasure is derived from development of an elegant solution to a complex problem. The joys and pains of creativity and learning in this context are intermingled. The emphasis on self-improvement and attainment of a high level of expertise are part of the meritocratic basis that constitutes the social organization of the FL/OSS movement. Participation in FL/OSS is often framed in terms of apprenticeship in the craft of programming, in which quality and the ability to 'make things work' are testament to an individual's abilities. For instance, Advogato, a peer-certification project for FL/OSS developers developed by a FL/OSS contributor, categorizes members as apprentices, journeymen and masters.

Like apprentices, new developers are often expected to start to develop their skills by initially undertaking more routine, secondary tasks. As their expertise develops, 'newbies' (individuals who have recently joined a project) are expected to move up the project hierarchy and assume greater responsibility and authority. This view of learning and organization is consistent with the CoP approach, a theoretical perspective described in Chapter 2, that is often adopted to account for FL/OSS community organization. Integral to this theory is the concept of practice, which is used to explain how collectives actually function—not according to the rulebook, but mostly based on making it up as they go along. The CoP perspective was developed to account for forms of learning that take place outside the contexts of formal education such as learning by doing and learning on the job. The theory suggests that as new members or legitimate peripheral learners adopt the community's methods and practices, they move from the periphery to the centre.

Availability of source code, the ability to 'look under the bonnet' to find out things, the open character of participation and the fact that, in principle, nobody is excluded are often regarded as key enablers of participation and learning in FL/OSS. However, the reality may be different. Mature FL/OSS projects involve thousands of lines of code and have complex architectures that are not always well documented. FL/OSS developers, as we have seen, use an array of specialized tools, such as VCS, and have to abide by formal and informal norms, processes and conventions that relate to the complex character of FL/OSS as a collaborative, software development effort.

The stumbling blocks to participation in FL/OSS that emerged through my five in-depth interviews with experienced programmers[1] and five interviews with new contributors to the GNOME and KDE communities can be categorized as follows. First, there are difficulties associated with the depth of understanding of the elements of development required before anyone can actually start 'fiddling' with the code. Second, there are conceptual difficulties related to acquiring an understanding of the program architecture, the development process workflow, the available sources of information and how they combine, and the network of people involved. Third, there are issues related to where newbies situate themselves in the development process—where they start and how they undertake tasks most appropriate to their skill levels.

Let us look at what each of these types of difficulties entails. Before they can begin to work with the code, new developers have to learn how to download (check out), build and install the program's sources. This allows them to run the latest in-production versions, a prerequisite for participation in the ongoing development process.[2] Installing this development snapshot is far from straightforward and constitutes a major impediment to new developers as it implies a familiarity with the tools and a non-trivial level of technical expertise. Some projects are trying to alleviate this problem by developing tools that create automated scripts for this process. For example, in 2008 GNOME released a kit for developers which allows programmers very quickly to compile the latest development snapshot of the project.

Once this initial hurdle is overcome, a newbie can begin to write patches, that is, to make comparatively small changes to the code base. This involves consideration of a number of issues, some of which are related to general good programming practice and some of which are project specific. They include writing a set of rules that will allow the submitted code to be built along with the rest of the sources, file-naming conventions, how to document changes, preferred styles for code writing, appropriate ways to modify other people's code, and some more specific project requirements. GNOME and KDE, for example, require developers to annotate code so that onscreen messages can be located and translated easily. This facilitates the process of 'localization' to different user language communities. This knowledge, as one interviewee pointed out, forms part of a broader conceptual understanding of 'how things fit and are put together' which newbies need to acquire. Modularity, the separation of a system into several components, does not entirely alleviate the need to understand the logic according to which the system is designed, or its dependencies; the different parts are meant to work together to support the whole. Moreover, there are elements of the software development process itself that need to be understood such as the type of changes that are permitted during each phase of the release process. Thus, technical merit is only one of the requirements for making a patch or more substantial changes for integration into the main development tree.

Some of these issues can be addressed by documentation. The provision of updated information on technical specifications that are continuously evolving is a constant challenge for FL/OSS projects. Because the provision of up-to-date material is not always possible, new developers are expected to develop an understanding of where to locate the latest information on the aspects of the project in which they are interested. This is rendered more difficult by the fragmented character of the available sources of information and the different elements of development. Neal, a relatively new contributor to the GNOME project at the time of the interviews, described this difficulty:

> Yeah, I think if you, to get involved into the thing its really hard I think, because basically everything is very disparate and you have the bug database here, you have the CVS access there, and there is no central documentation for how to get involved into all this and you have to learn by yourself all the different entry points, you have to learn that you have to read the mailing lists, that you have to read the CVS commit to stay aware of what is happening, you have to read different websites, but, all these information sources are set up by people who know each other, so every time something new happens, everybody in their little circle is aware of it. But for outsiders it is very hard to stay, to stay in front of everything, you have to keep looking everywhere and notice new stuff and just go there and take a look. It has been better recently, because of all the websites and Planet GNOME is very useful for that, because it centralizes the whole development information, but you still have to read everything and take out what is really important and throw out all the personal stuff, so, I think that it is a lot of work, but at the same time, it is really interesting, so it is not really that bad. (19.10.04)

The challenges that Neal talks about are associated with the difficulty of acquiring a conceptual understanding of the development process and constructing a frame of reference for situating and keeping track of developments.

The intertwining of the social and the technical aspects of the information highlighted by Neal is a key dimension of this process. Acquiring an understanding of the community and of who is responsible for what is essential in order to identify who it is that can provide the answer to a query or help with a specific problem. Some knowledge, often described as 'sticky' knowledge (Brown and Duguid, 2000), as is the case in more traditional organizations, cannot be captured without substantial cost. In the case of sticky knowledge, the cost is based on the effort required from newbies to familiarize themselves with the network of FL/OSS contributors and to start building cooperative relationships that will support their efforts. There is also a clear distinction between 'know how' and 'know who'. An individual may have very substantial skills (know how), but be unable to employ them effectively in the social context of the development process because of lack of social integration. 'Know who' is not only about the linkages among individuals; it also includes effective exchange of the contextualized knowledge required to introduce ideas into a collective or collaborative process. These relational, social aspect of FL/OSS are reminiscent of the problems that arise from the embedded character of participation which initiatives such as the GNOME Bounty Hunt have sought to address.

Another hurdle for new contributors is finding a suitable task. Eight out of the ten interviewees who were asked about the barriers to learning in FL/OSS considered this to be a major step towards becoming a recognized contributor. Flint, a newbie coder, was of the opinion that having tasks or projects explicitly addressed to new developers facilitated participation greatly, not least because the initiators of such tasks usually acted as mentors. All the newbies interviewed placed high value on mentoring relationships because of the learning they facilitated and the reassurance they provided that their efforts were appreciated. Although responsiveness is often cited as one of the key characteristics of FL/OSS, getting the right person to pay attention and provide constructive feedback on the work done is not always straightforward. Despite—and in some cases because of—these difficulties, my interviewees described their experience of participation and collaboration in FL/OSS as a sustained learning experience.

The five in-depth interviews with senior developers,[3] however, provide a very different view. They emphasized the goal and results-oriented character of the development process which seems to shape their expectations with regard to the behaviour and performance of newbies and influences their decisions about whether or not to help them.

One of the characteristics most valued in new contributors—and FL/OSS development in general—is self-reliance. Nine of my interviewees referred to self-reliance as one of the most important characteristics for a new developer. The ability independently to navigate the maze of FL/OSS projects and find answers is connected to two main factors in FL/OSS development. The first is the availability of source code, which is seen as the ultimate, crucial documentation. Access to the source code means that potentially most questions, in principle, can be answered. The second is the limited time available to senior developers in an intensive production oriented environment to teach others. The rapid release rate of FL/OSS developments, and the fact that many developers work on a volunteer basis, makes time a very scarce resource in FL/OSS communities. Every minute helping a newbie may be a minute spent not writing code. The high turnover in contributors, combined with programmers who say that they want to help and then disappear, makes senior developers cautious about choosing whom to invest their time in.

One of the first things that all the interviewees stressed as important for assessing the potential of new contributors was the chosen entry point and their initial introduction on the mailing lists. This is what Sebastian, a senior KDE developer, had to say:

> Yeah, you realize that from the first step he takes. If he is like coming to mailing lists saying, hey, how can I help, that's the kind of people that are not going to follow up and I am actually on the how to help alias for KDE org, so I get all those mails from people that say, hey, how could I help and one percent remains up there, even though I try to provide very helpful answers and guide them to what they could do, they don't go anywhere, because those people assume that there is an easy answer to a question of how can I help and that someone is going to teach them everything and that's not how it works, because no one is going to take the time to do that. On the other hand if you see someone coming to a mailing list with already a patch to fix something or you feel from his questions that he has really looked into things deeply, then you know that it is going to be someone who is going to be efficient and that you can spend a bit of time helping that person. (23.08.04)

Sam, another senior KDE developer, described the rule of thumb that experienced developers employ in assessing the level of commitment of new developers:

> I think that most of the time, its not as immediate, so, you can't talk to them once and tell whether they are going to stay around, but if they, its very obvious if someone shows up and then in the first two weeks you start to see productive results out of them, you can say, ok, its worth to invest more time in this person, they are looking like they are regularly contributing things back or having some sort of sustained productive output, whereas there are some people, some people very much like the idea of being an open source developer, but they are not willing to put the work into it and its a lot of work. (14.04.04)

Martin, a GNOME developer, pointed out that, ideally, new participants should pass through the peripheral participation stage rapidly, discreetly and almost invisibly:

No, new developers that come along, the good developers suddenly appear on the scene as if they had been working on the stuff for years. They will have figured all this stuff out very, very quickly and I suppose it is this kind of developers that we really want to attract. So we are not trying to really attract, people who are not capable of going off and figuring out stuff for themselves. So it is almost like a baptism of fire, you just sink or you swim, so it might be a little bit cruel, but the amount of effort that would be required for an existing developer to bring a new developer up to speed who isn't capable of bringing himself up to speed, you might not get a good developer out in the end, at the other end, which is, you know what I mean? (11.07.04)

Martin's comment indicates how intertwined the values of self-reliance, commitment and productivity can be. Putting in the time and effort required to find answers for oneself is an indication of commitment and a prerequisite for sustained participation. Successful information seekers and dedicated learners do not impose on the time and attention of senior developers. Self-reliance in learning attests to the potential of newbies to evolve into productive contributors. Although the importance of learning in FL/OSS was acknowledged, apprenticeship or peripheral participation is meant to be a solitary activity that takes place in the background, not at the forefront of developments.

One interviewee mentioned the importance of designing learning activities that involve coordination with developers to ensure that they fit into existing routines. This interviewee cited the successful example of KDE 'junior jobs', an initiative that encourages maintainers to identify bugs submitted to the bugs database as suitable for new contributors to work on. Also, Sebastian indicated that seasoned developers can usually judge the potential of new contributors very quickly, sometimes even after their first couple of postings. How potential contributors introduce themselves to the community is related to how successfully they have assimilated the behavioural 'scripts' (von Krogh et al., 2003), which are the norms and values of FL/OSS development, and a newbie's initial postings usually indicate the extent of their commitment to the development process. This suggests that newbies are expected to have assimilated a great deal through reading and observation before they start developing, which might account for the practice of 'lurking' on project mailing lists.[4] The public, archival character of mailing lists and their use as repositories of knowledge makes the posting of messages a non-trivial affair, especially for new developers.

But the production-oriented character of FL/OSS and the emphasis placed on the delivery of quality outputs, coupled with the pressures of commercialization, can have a negative impact on participation. In his keynote speech to GUADEC 2004, Nat Friedman commented on the barriers to participation and innovation in FL/OSS. He suggested that the FL/OSS culture had become intolerant of newbies and that the barriers to entry had become so high that they hindered the influx of new ideas and were compromising the future of the community. In order to overcome this problem some projects have set up tasks specifically addressed to new contributors. For example, the Google Summer of Code is a contest that offers money prizes to students for participation in FL/OSS projects, which is an attempt to address this problem systematically. Although the contest has been running since 2005 and has involved many projects, how successful it has been in attracting long-term contributors is not yet known.

Are these efforts to lower the barriers to participation going against senior developers' views that the collection of difficulties that newbies face is an essential selection mechanism? These different perspectives perhaps express tension between the desire to maintain a high level of technical quality and the need to facilitate access, which is based on the limited resources of FL/OSS, the objective difficulties of visualizing decentralized development, and the problems involved in balancing collectivist and individual demands such as in sharing and excelling.

There may be another explanation. It may be that these perspectives are contradictory only if we retain a view of periphery activity as a preparatory stage for the core. Lakhani (2006) draws attention to the value of the periphery, defined in this case as the body of programmers outside the core project team, for problem solving and feature innovation. This value emerges not necessarily through the provision of ready-made solutions, but through the periphery's role in sustaining a productive dialogue with the core. It is plausible that senior developers' views and the activities that lead to accumulated learning express two overlapping, but distinct, dimensions of learning. In the first instance, facilitating learning is designed to lower the barriers to participation for potentially productive[5] peripheral programmers and to sustain an image of a welcoming and accessible community. For senior developers, the goal is to identify newbies who will be able to undertake work on the more critical parts of development and eventually move to the core.

NOT EVERYTHING IS ABOUT PROGRAMMING: AUTONOMOUS PERIPHERALITY IN FL/OSS

There is another view of the periphery that relates to the activities that complement and support code development in FL/OSS projects. Some of these tasks are associated with the administration and maintenance of the technical and organizational infrastructures of projects. These include website maintenance (including wikis, blog aggregators, etc.), administration of development tools such as VCSs, bugs databases and their associated contributor accounts, management of different aspects of membership and their supporting processes. Many of these tasks are performed by individuals or specially appointed groups and, although routine in nature, involve a high level of responsibility. Achieving the right to modify content on the primary project websites which convey the principal image of the community is a lot more difficult than obtaining write access to the code base.

Other supporting tasks involve coordination of the development process. In GNOME, for example, coordination of releases historically has been managed by a release team, whereas in KDE the task of implementing the release schedule is usually the responsibility of one individual—the release 'dude'. Communities sometimes experiment with different governance schemes in which governance is defined as the accumulation of decision-making authority. KDE's no-longer-functioning technical working group, for example, was based on an elected group of individuals responsible for defining and executing official KDE software releases, providing advice on technical decisions and maintaining the development process.[6] In contrast, management of the projects' legal and funding activities, including relations with non-profit and for-profit organizations, is managed by the GNOME Foundation and KDE e.V. These roles and activities emerge from the continuous growth and increasing adoption of FL/OSS.

There is yet another view of the periphery that involves activities apart from low- or high-level routine development and organizational tasks. In the contexts of the KDE and GNOME projects, these tasks involve artists, translators, documenters, usability and accessibility experts, and individuals who assist with marketing and public relations. It is helpful to group these aspects of contribution under the term 'autonomous peripherality'. Autonomous stresses the distinctive nature of these activities, distinguishing them from the idea of periphery described thus far, and especially from *legitimate* peripheral participation, which refers to a stage in the apprenticeship phase of community members. I examine the idea of autonomous peripherality by considering the organization of the translation and documentation teams, their make-up, values and agendas, and how they cooperate with programmers. My evidence is based on 11 in-depth interviews with contributors engaged in autonomous peripheral tasks and related initiatives and the results of my survey of the members of the GNOME Foundation and KDE e.V. These data were used to illustrate the effects of employment on participation described in Chapter 5.

The scale of some (autonomous) peripheral activities is surprising. The GNOME and KDE translator communities, for example, are of similar size and intensity to the programmers' group. Both communities have more than 50 translator teams generating translations from English, to German, to Welsh, to Swahili, and so on. The documenter teams are smaller and usually involve a handful of dedicated contributors.

The organization of the translator teams resembles that of coding teams, but with some important differences. In both KDE and GNOME, every language team has a leader whose role is similar to that of a maintainer. Language team leaders are responsible for correcting mistakes and reviewing and integrating different parts of the translations, ensuring consistency in terms of agreed terminology. Internationalization projects include a coordinator with responsibility for organizing new language teams and liaising between coders and translators. And whereas modules may have more than one maintainer, language teams have only one team leader and usually only a few people with CVS commit privileges.

KDE and GNOME have tried to establish the notion that participation in autonomous peripheral tasks is a valuable form of contribution. Both communities have tried to lower the barriers to participation by minimizing the level of technical skill required and by automating and organizing the process to a degree that, in theory, even people with no knowledge of Linux or Unix could contribute to the internationalization effort. Both projects have developed specialized translation tools, devised by programmers interested in promoting localization, such KBabel and Localize. Project websites provide extensive information on different aspects of peripheral development, including workflow of the translation process and suggestions about how to become involved or how to introduce a new language. However, the expectations associated with peripheral tasks compared to code development, create some problems in ensuring the quality of contributions. This is what Ken, a leading figure on the KDE documentation team, had to say on this issue:

> Yeah, a lot of people don't want to make any kind of commitment. They want to do something one time, get their buzz that they helped out on a open source project, I am cool and that's it, they don't ever want to see it again and that's fine with me (laughs). If the content is good. It seems to me that those kind of people are sometimes more trouble than they're worth because they are also the ones that tend to dust something off in five minutes without putting a lot of thought into it and it is quite sloppy and needs editing and massaging to be put into the document and then when you say that to them or you send a draft back for them to check over they are like, God, I gave you this thing for free, just put it in the user manual. Your user manuals are terrible, you need my help! Yeah, they are doing us a big favour, but well, they are really not, if their five minute contribution takes an hour of work from my part to shape into something we can actually use, I may as well have written that myself. (01.10.04)

The data from my study do not enable me to draw systematic conclusions about the skill sets of peripheral developers or provide information to establish whether Ken's view is shared by programmers and non-programmers. Of the 12 peripheral contributors I interviewed, 5 were programmers. One was engaged in translation related to code development; another thought that translation work was a better use of his time than programming; a third chose to split his time between coding and assisting with usability issues.

Although the picture of the skills profiles of peripheral contributors and their career paths within the projects is unclear, there are some important indications with regard to their employment status. Table 6.1 presents the responses from the members of the GNOME Foundation and KDE e.V. to show how volunteers and contributors hired to work on projects were distributed according to their reported main areas of contribution. Table 6.1 shows that 64.7% of peripheral activities are undertaken by volunteers. The peripheral activities performed by employed contributors include mainly organizational tasks such as involvement in the two projects' principal organizational bodies. The associations between participation types and tasks are statistically significant (χ2 (df=3, N=262)= 19.38, p.<.05). The adjusted residual for peripheral activities (2.7) shown in Table 6.1, which identifies the most important patterns of contribution, suggests that being a volunteer is positively associated with being involved in peripheral activities and negatively associated with code contributions to the core infrastructure modules of development.

Table 6.1　Relationship between Affiliation and Area of Contribution

		Primary modules	Secondary modules	Development tools and tasks	Peripheral activities	Total
Volunteers	Count	29	49	10	44	132
	% within Group	22.00%	37.10%	7.60%	33.30%	100.00%
	% within Area	34.10%	59.80%	37.00%	64.70%	50.40%
	Adjusted Residual	-3.6	2	-1.5	2.7	
Employed to work in the project	Count	56	33	17	24	130
	% within Group	43.10%	25.40%	13.10%	18.50%	100.00%
	% within Area	65.90%	40.20%	63.00%	35.30%	49.60%
	Adjusted Residual	3.6	-2	1.5	-2.7	
Total	Count	85	82	27	68	262

Source: GNOME Foundation and KDE e.V. survey, N=262

Are there any other differences between individuals involved mainly in development and those involved in translation and documentation? Ten out of 11 of the autonomous peripheral contributors interviewed described themselves as users and insisted that their work was more practically oriented than that of programmers. They said that their activities were directed to facilitating access and dissemination rather than directly promoting development. Eight long-term peripheral contributors were not interested in coding. This is what Ken, a leading documenter and translator in the KDE project, had to say:

> It is because we are users, much more than the developers, we are the ones that open every single application and look at every dialogue, we are the ones that actually have to use them, and it is also the main impetus for the translators to get involved, it is because they want to use the software in their own language. Most of translators, that's the main reason that they are doing it. We tend to be a lot less of the hardcore free software kind of people. Most of us are doing it for really practical reasons, that's a simple way to put it and I am generalizing. (24.08.04)

Another visible difference lies in the implications of the work requirements of translators and documenters. To ensure that all the elements of applications are translated or documented correctly, these groups have to use the particular applications. This allows them a global view of the project. Sean, a translator in GNOME who previously was involved in bug tracking, described the implications of working in the periphery:

> I think contributing on the periphery, not in the code, means that you end up with a better overview and understanding of the project as a whole and, for example, if you are going to Bugzilla, even if you think that you are only looking for bugs in the file manager. One bug that you deal with may be related to underlying libraries and how they deal with information and so you learn about that and then the next bug may be related to the look of the thing and you will have to go and look at the human interface guidelines, which are the usability aspect and so you learn about that and similarly you go through proof reading documentation or translating strings and you look at a string perhaps and say 'Oh, wow, I have got to translate that, what program is this?' And you will often look and you realize that you had no idea that that program could do that and you learn this about all the programs, not just this that you are coding on. I have seen discussions on the mailing lists about, I think that it would be great to add this kind of functionality to this application, says somebody who works on this application and then somebody else would say. Why? We already have it over here on this one. So I think that at the edge, you get a much rounder, overall picture of all the little bits going on. (09.03.04)

It is interesting to compare this view with the difficulties experienced by newbies in developing a conceptual understanding of how the different parts of the project relate to the whole and to relate this to each group's work pattern. It has been suggested, for example, that most programmers usually concentrate on a few modules (Ghosh and David, 2003). In other words, they are specialists. Due to the nature of their work, however, translators more regularly engage with aspects of the project that are exposed to users than most programmers, but this type of input is not systematically employed in most projects. For example, although translators are ideal beta testers, there is a general view that most do not submit regular bug reports even for stable releases. This could be due to a lack of interest on the part of many translators in participating actively in (code) development. On the other hand, it could be due to the level of technical knowledge required to compile programs from their sources which, as indicated, is a prerequisite for participating in real-time development and is required to report bugs in a technically precise manner. Or it could be because translators' patterns of work and collaboration tend to be intensive and seasonal.

The case of documenters is slightly different as more sophisticated skills are required for technical writing. Documenters in FL/OSS have the difficult task of producing information suitable for, potentially, very different end-user audiences and prospective developers. Also, documenters often cooperate closely with developers of project modules, who may have documented some aspects, but often not to the standards required. Although significant efforts are made in GNOME and KDE to make bug reports and mailing lists accessible through search engines, this information is not usually integrated in project documentation. This seems to be due mostly to the small number of regular volunteer documenters who are working in these projects.

The differences between the coding and the autonomous peripheral community suggested in other studies (Studer, 2007) is reinforced by the few opportunities for exchanges between coders and non-coders. Despite the existence of a main internationalization mailing list and the requirement for team leaders to follow its postings, coders frequently complain that it is difficult to get messages through to translators. Ken, a KDE contributor, who was involved primarily in documentation, but with considerable experience in translating, commented on the problems of communication between the two communities and stressed the importance of having a coordinator, someone who could straddle the boundaries of these groups:

> I think that is actually a problem; we used to have Thomas Diehl, being the guy between and he has definitely stepped back and nobody has taken up his place, to actually, this is what I do for the docs, it is my job, its just getting in there and talking to people to relay messages back and the translation team could really benefit from somebody doing that, because the developers just don't think, don't remember to

ask the translators and the translators seem to sit in their little ghetto on the mailing lists and complain about things to each other but don't actually go to the developer and every time it happens, some random person will tell the developer, there was a really big problem with the application and they come on the mailing lists and say, oh my god I am so sorry what can I do to fix it and it is immediately fixable and I think having a coordinator would really help but it is a big job and it really needs someone who is really willing to put in a lot of time to step up and do it. (1.10.04)

The particular problem that Ken refers to occurs when programmers fail to mark up (to designate in the agreed format for the project) the strings of the code that are visible to the user and require translation. Translators use specialized tools in order to extract these translatable strings and compile the special (.po) files that are used for translations. To finalize their work, translators need to re-integrate the translated strings into the development tree. If the strings to be translated are not properly marked up, the translators cannot do their work. This is a basic requirement that coders must take into account when writing applications.

Another practice that has been developed to accommodate the needs of the internationalization project is that of 'string freezing'. This is the last in a series of accumulative freezes[7] and generally involves a period of two to three weeks prior to a new release, during which time hackers are not allowed to make any changes that might affect the string of messages in the code that is visible to users. This allows translators to catch up, complete and update translations of the messages which, up to that time, have been changing as the applications that contained them were continuously worked on. This period also allows documenters to finalize their documentation of new features and any other improvements to the code base. Thus, unlike coders who can work more or less continuously on the project, translators are seasonal workers whose involvement in the development process may be for only a couple of weeks before a major release, during which time the bulk of their work is accomplished.

The imposition of a string freeze on coders is not unproblematic. Knowing that there is still some time before the release during which, in theory, enhancements could be made to a program, is frustrating to many coders. However, communities do make provisions for string-freezes to be broken to allow developers to make alterations to their programs within this period. It involves the developer(s) making a case to the coordinator of the translator team and the release team (GNOME) or the release dude (KDE) about why their proposed changes are necessary. In both projects, decisions are made on a case-by-case basis, but it is not always clear who actually authorizes a string-freeze breakage.

Most translators and coders involved in the internationalization project seem to think that, despite the progress made in accommodating the needs of translators, because of the relatively low importance ascribed to peripheral activities compared to contributing code, programmers need to be reminded constantly about their existence and the necessity for their involvement. Although the contributions of non-coders are becoming better appreciated,[8] 11 of my interviewees saw programming as undoubtedly the most valuable form of contribution and developers as usually having the most say in the development process. Al, a developer in the GNOME project, elaborated,

> To a certain extent in a lot of open source projects and in GNOME, it is definitely true that the people who contribute the code are the people who get to decide what happens. Now this kind of may lead to some technical citizenry in that the people who do the graphics or the people who do the documentation do have to work quite a lot harder to be seen as a really key contributor who can help make decisions and I don't think that there are many, [the] people you would include in listings as core developers would be someone who wrote documentation or did artwork or something like that, which may, well I guess you might say, well they are not developers but they certainly have a role to play there. (24.06.04)

To sum up, cooperation between coders and translators is highly modular, and communication between them is fragmented. This is the result of a lack of interest on the part of the two groups in the other's work and a consequence of the way the internationalization effort is organized. With a few exceptions, documenters and translators are involved in the development process only at certain periods when the work of the coders is on hold. In contrast to programmers, translators and documenters see themselves more as users, emphasizing the importance of access and usability.

SITUATING AND ORGANIZING PERIPHERAL PARTICIPATION

Whereas attracting new developers is critical for all stages of FL/OSS community growth, how to encourage and better organize autonomous peripheral participation seems to be more closely associated with the evolution of FL/OSS ties with the wider user and developer bases. As FL/OSS becomes increasingly incorporated in non-technical production environments—that is, through exploitation on home and office desktops—the need to understand and support non-technical users also increases. Although this is considered to be primarily the purview of FL/OSS companies and one of the main aspects of their business models, communities are showing growing interest in involving non-coders in development. In addition to addressing more directly the requirements of the non-technical user base, this interest is also related to the desire to signal a strong sense of community and the maturity and user-friendliness of the project.

The large-scale deployment of FL/OSS in companies and public organizations is making these issues more pressing. Communities have experimented with methods for supporting and organizing autonomous peripheral activities. The case study I draw on here is of KDE Quality Teams, an initiative aimed at creating a supportive, non-coding community around the various KDE platform applications. It consists of four in-depth interviews with participants in the initiative and analysis of online materials.

The idea of KDE Quality Teams (http://quality.kde.org/) was introduced in 2003 by Leonhard Carlos Woeltz, a trade investment consultant who became involved in FL/OSS because of his belief in its potential for developing countries. Woeltz initially conceived the role of KDE Quality Teams, originally called Janitors, as follows:

> The main idea is to create a community based quality team of non-developers, that would focus on the whole of individual modules of applications, working orthogonally to developers, documenters, users and testers, instead of the specific of the whole. In other words think of acting upon the whole of Kontact instead of acting upon the what's this of KDE project. The key idea is attracting people in a way that's both interesting to them and more useful to KDE project. This would be the basis of a community oriented (instead of company oriented) effort of improving this experience. We have a wonderful community, kde-look.org, KDE wiki and all the translating teams are strong evidence of this.[9]

The objective of KDE Quality Teams was to organize the increasing non-programmer involvement in KDE in a better way, by creating a support group around each application in the form of a team of contributors that would provide help the maintainers in the areas of design, user interface and documentation. The local character of these teams and their focus on a single project were expected to provide a clearer direction and improve the 'social experience' of participation.[10] The desire for a community rather than a corporate-based initiative is indicative of a desire to maintain the grassroots character of peripheral activities. These activities were seen as having the potential to enhance the appeal of non-coding group involvement, often seen as an indication of the strong sense of community of such projects and, thus, as valuable for attracting new volunteers—coders and non-coders.

Although the KDE community welcomed KDE Quality Teams, the project faced a number of challenges which changed its original orientation. One of the main problems faced by its founding members was the difficulty of communicating the objectives of Quality teams in a clear manner. Many potential contributors thought that membership of one of these teams required expertise in documentation, artwork and usability. Another problem was related to the time and effort required to set up the teams: many potential volunteers were discouraged by the sheer amount of work involved. KDE was able to create only a few quality teams, the most notable being the KDE Personal Information Management Quality Team, whose success depended largely on the presence and continuous efforts of one individual, Leonhard Carlos Woeltz. There was a third challenge which was related to eliciting the help of coders in the creation and maintenance of task lists.

However, the project focus soon shifted and team members prioritized activities towards supporting new contributors. KDE Quality Teams gradually became conduits and first points of contact for new contributors to become familiarized with the structure of the project. Help for newbies—coders and non-coders—came in the form of documentation and guidance provided through the KDE Quality Team mailing list.

GNOME also has a mailing list—GNOME-love—which is dedicated to newbies' queries. Quality teams were set up to act as umbrellas for groups of activities, as in the KDE Usability Project, but developed into separate projects. The situation surrounding usability changed dramatically following the involvement of Relevantive AG (http://www.relevantive.de/), a German-based usability company that offered pro bono services to the KDE and other FL/OSS projects. Relevantive created an initiative called the Open Usability project, a FL/OSS multimedia framework project (http://openusability.org/projects/kde-hig/) that provided a variety of services, including direct expert advice to maintainers, to improve the user interface of their applications. The involvement of this specialist company in usability seems to have alleviated many of the problems faced by maintainers.

In an interview in 2004 which predated Relevantive AG's involvement, Dean, a KDE coder, described the challenges related to usability and the problems involved in participation of non-coders in the development process:

> A lot of the time when we are designing interfaces, in the past we were able to design them from the point of view of how the technical person drives this, and what is changing now is we need to much more take into account how a non technical person drives it, but we need to do that without upsetting the technical people.

> Interviewer: Well, that's tricky.

> Dean: Yes, it is very hard, the problem is that the technical people are likely to be the people who would be the next generation of developers who [are] taken on board. To say that they don't like the project, we don't get any new developers and ultimately the project will fail. We have a difficult balance to strike and at the moment, you know, that's one of the big questions in KDE and if you look at KDE developers.org, the sort of the web blog site, you find that there is a lot of discussion going on about how we can manage this process and integrate teams of people who are trying to improve the user interface with the teams of

people who are trying to develop the system without everybody shout-
ing at each other and eventually storming off. (22.03.04)

Dean's comments highlight two issues central to the organization of autonomous peripheral participation in FL/OSS. The first relates to the question of how to involve the non-technical community without alienating
the 'techies'. The second relates to how to improve cooperation between
them. The KDE Quality Teams and the Open Usability project provided
two very different solutions to these problems. The more local character of
the KDE Quality Teams, with their focus on individual applications rather
than on the whole of the project, was based on a holistic approach aimed
at encompassing a wide range of activities within the context of the same
sub-project. Also, the initiative was addressed to anyone who wanted to
become involved, regardless of experience or expertise. The Open Usability
project had a narrower focus, but the professional credentials of its initiators helped to diffuse subjective arguments about what would improve user
experience, and the provision of consulting services on a case-by-case basis
was less intrusive for maintainers. Lastly, whereas KDE Quality Teams was
a specific KDE initiative, the Open Usability project provided its platform
and services to all interested FL/OSS developers.

THE CORE AND PERIPHERY REVISITED: FL/OSS
COMMUNITIES AS CONSTELLATIONS OF PRACTICE

The focus on the software engineering aspects of FL/OSS and its impact on
the practices of the software industry allow little room for considering the
importance of autonomous peripheral participation. This in part is because
non-coding peripheral activities, such as usability and documentation, that
are relevant to a large number of FL/OSS projects are usually considered
secondary to the development of a working code base. The deficiency of
FL/OSS projects in these areas is frequently tied to some perceived characteristics of the FL/OSS model of development and organization. These
characteristics include the low status assigned to these tasks in the context
of projects (a view held by several interviewees) which discourages programmers from undertaking them.

It is also in part due to the fact that these responsibilities are usually
seen as an element of FL/OSS dissemination rather than an integral part of
the development process. They are often regarded as a luxury rather than
a necessity and come to the fore only when the code base has achieved
a certain level of technical maturity. The underlying assumption is that
community-founded and -governed FL/OSS communities have limited
resources which can only be diverted to secondary activities when projects have been proven to be technically viable. There is another important distinction, between peripheral activities geared towards end-users

and those addressed to developers (both types of audiences may overlap, especially in more technical projects, such as the programming language Perl). In this case developer documentation is considered crucial for the recruitment of new volunteers. Commercially initiated FL/OSS projects, such as IBM's Eclipse development platform, provide extensive documentation in the hope of attracting external contributions. The development of documentation is ingrained in many firms' FL/OSS business models. The publisher O'Reilly, for example, generates a large number of FL/OSS user and technical guides.

The importance of autonomous peripheral contributions in FL/OSS should be viewed more broadly than is suggested by a comparison of the strengths and weaknesses of proprietary and the community-driven FL/OSS models of development. Their significance is associated with the ability of FL/OSS to mobilize and organize types of expertise other than coding, on the one hand, and its role in promoting access, on the other. The mobilization of other types of expertise than programming, such as those relevant to the knowledge domain of the software, has been somewhat neglected by researchers due to the infrastructure focus in early successful FL/OSS projects, which were addressed primarily to the technical programmer and systems administrator communities. Furthermore, attention to issues such as the user interface and accessibility has frequently been considered to be part of the added value that companies appropriating returns from FL/OSS, such as those selling commercial FL/OSS distributions, bring to the equation.

Nevertheless, as the FL/OSS community develops more solutions for more diverse and specialized communities of users, such as health professionals, scientists and educators, the importance of autonomous peripheral contributions will increase. This dimension has been neglected in approaches that emphasize the importance of FL/OSS as a user-driven innovation. In highlighting the different aspects of FL/OSS that different groups choose to prioritize, this discussion introduces the notion of what constitutes a user in FL/OSS. Almost all the peripheral contributors I interviewed, many of whom where programmers, emphasized access and ease of use over technical excellence. The challenges faced by these teams include how the input provided by the non-technical groups is valued and incorporated in FL/OSS developments and how such decisions are implemented in project workflows.

FL/OSS communities are experimenting with many different solutions. Some, for example, KDE Quality Teams, are directed to providing in-house answers by developing the project's own capabilities, others are experimenting with creating specialized actors, as in the case of the Open Usability project, to service multiple projects. In developing capabilities in areas of expertise relevant to their knowledge domains, project participants can sometimes benefit from cooperation with companies. For example, historically, GNOME's accessibility program has benefited from cooperation with developers from Sun Microsystems Inc. which, in its turn, exploits the community's translation efforts.[11]

The significance of the accessibility, localization and translation efforts in GNOME and KDE is associated with the wider role of FL/OSS in promoting access by addressing the needs of minority groups which cannot be fulfilled by proprietary alternatives due to prohibitive costs or under-provision in the market. This aspect of FL/OSS can also be viewed from the perspective of its role as an instrument of economic development policy at both regional and national levels. Countries such as Brazil and South Africa have embraced FL/OSS as the preferred platform for their public administration, education and e-government services. In 2005, for example, some of the government ministries in Brazil announced that their systems would be switching to GNU/Linux.[12]

The thread connecting autonomous peripheral participation with learning is indicative of how the requirements for open access are balanced with those of quality—here defined as technical quality. My examination of the challenges faced by new developers and the expectations of senior developers reveals how demanding is the process of learning. Studies relating to learning in FL/OSS usually focus on aspects of socialization and integration in the norms and values of the community. However, the difficulties arising as a result of the decentralized and socially embedded character of collaboration, as well as the demands of continuous production and the tensions between the collectivist and individualist aspects of participation, also need consideration. These shape a framework of participation in which independence, value and self-initiative are appreciated and where the time and attention of senior developers must be earned. The process of learning is as much a process of enculturation as a process of integration into a professional network; it is a process of familiarization with a specific software methodology and a code base.

I have suggested that community attempts to lower the barriers to participation for new developers should not be seen as contradicting senior developers' views that learning serves as a (necessary) selection mechanism. These attitudes may include two overlapping, but distinct, dimensions. In allowing their involvement in secondary coding activities, such as bug tracking and testing, or the occasional submission of small code contributions, the efforts to lower the barriers to participation are very important for developers who otherwise might remain at the periphery of the programming community. The interest of senior developers is directed towards those developers who are able to make more substantial contributions and may eventually move to the core. In many cases, the advantages of large numbers of peripheral programmers forms an important part of the added value that companies often see FL/OSS as providing.

This aspect of the periphery is especially important when viewed in the light of the results concerning the types of contributors and affiliations, where the majority of maintainers is shown to be employed to work on projects whose secondary activities are driven primarily by volunteers.

The picture that emerges is one of FL/OSS communities as multi-layered, consisting of groups of contributors with different priorities, views and agendas. FL/OSS communities are constellations of practice, joined by a project's overarching goals, but distinctive in their priorities, rhythms of development and patterns of collaboration. The division and relationship between core and periphery that has been proposed as the schema that best captures the emergent organization of FL/OSS (David and Rullani, 2008; Koch and Schneider, 2002; Lakhani, 2006) and other peer-driven projects (Kittur et al., 2007) need to be re-examined and elaborated in the light of the evidence offered in this and the preceding chapter. Conceptions of the core and periphery would benefit from quantitative and qualitative investigation which would broaden the types of tasks and levels of expertise of the project participants examined.

Autonomous and legitimate peripheral participation are important considerations because they reflect the challenges that emerge in FL/OSS projects as they grow and reach larger audiences. FL/OSS projects need continuously to improve their capacity to recruit new capable members and balance quality and access. And they also must confront the problem of how to take advantage of different types of expertise that may challenge the conceptualization and function of FL/OSS projects as pure technical spaces.

7 The Story So Far
Technologies of Communities and Peer Production

The FL/OSS movement can be viewed as the improbable success of individuals and collectives in challenging existing institutions, reflecting their desire to operate in the market economy, but with a difference—that difference being the willingness to contribute freely to the creation of a public good. The FL/OSS model of organization is often seen as a template for work and the organization of commons-based peer or social production that can be transferred to other domains of intellectual work.[1] The FL/OSS movement is increasingly a story of transformation in which a new model of social production is incorporated into the strategy of dominant institutions and forms the basis for new ways of conducting business. Successful partnerships between firms and communities are used to showcases strategies, such as 'open innovation', for better exploitation of the 'commons'. Slowly, but steadily, attention is shifting away from understanding the gift and exchange economies as contrasting logics for coordinating and motivating action, and towards hybridity, with the objective of a successful synthesis.

This book examines the development of hybridity from several perspectives. Chapter 3 looked at the complex methodological issues involved in studying FL/OSS communities. The attempt to recover a coherent view of FL/OSS communities and FL/OSS development through the use of multiple data sources reveals that research of this type is as much about constructing as analysing a fixed phenomenon. Depending on which data are combined, and how and from what sources, slightly different views of FL/OSS emerge. The focus then shifted to two central aspects of the ongoing transformation of FL/OSS: the commercialization of FL/OSS software and the incorporation of FL/OSS communities into dominant market flows. Chapter 4 highlighted how firms use FL/OSS in order to generate revenue and to position themselves within networks of developers and other firms in order to expand their capacities to learn and innovate. Particular attention was directed to the factors that influence the ability of *corporately* initiated FL/OSS projects to mobilize and sustain external contributions. In Chapter 5 the perspective was reversed to encompass an investigation of the implications of commercialization for projects initiated and managed *independently* by firms. In Chapter 6, I discussed the implications of the growth of FL/OSS projects for the recruitment of volunteers and for aspects of contribution related to quality, usability and accessibility.

What conclusions can we draw from these findings about how FL/OSS communities are organized and the potential of the FL/OSS model of development to reconfigure relations among actors and change dominant practices and ways of thinking? At the beginning of this book I proposed a toolbox for ideas[2] that can be used to examine the evolution of FL/OSS and to assess its transformative potential as a new form of power. In this chapter, I reconnect the insights and findings presented in Chapter 6 to this original set of ideas in order to answer the question just posed. The first part of this chapter deals with the character of large FL/OSS communities as constellations of practice that are embedded in existing market dynamics. I emphasize the challenges that community-founded and -driven FL/OSS projects face as they grow and consolidate links with the market economy, and the ambiguous nature of the power relationships that develop among companies, individuals and firms.

A central idea of the theoretical toolkit is 'technologies of communities'. These technologies, which extend concepts borrowed from the work of Michel Foucault (1982b,c) and Nikolas Rose (1999), represent values, tools and processes that are crucial for establishing FL/OSS communities as subjects and objects of governance. The second part of this chapter explains how the different elements of technologies of communities help us to understand the broader implications of the FL/OSS model of organization and, in particular, its effect on reconfiguring the relationship between sociality and production.

THE AMBIGUITY OF EMBEDDEDNESS AND THE COMPLEXITY OF THE PERIPHERY

The idea of hybridity is becoming increasingly popular in explaining the new types of synergies that develop between firms and volunteer FL/OSS contributors and between the market and gift economies (Lessig, 2008; Lin, 2006; Shah, 2006, West, 2003). Although useful in signalling the advent of new varieties of communities, it cannot on its own describe which different configurations of interests they might adopt and who might gain or lose from any particular form. Nonetheless, there are some regularities. For example, it could be expected that corporately initiated FL/OSS projects would seek to maintain a balance between the gift and exchange economies that favours the interests of the sponsoring firm(s) in cases of conflict or disagreement with other participants. In particular, firm-sponsored efforts may be more willing to pull out of the development if such sacrifice be required, to achieve the degree of control desired by the sponsor over the pace and direction of projects initiated and managed at the grassroots level. Labelling mixed efforts hybrids without any further investigation can divert attention from the process through which different interests and agendas are aligned and negotiated, by implying the attainment of a fixed balance or unity between different agendas. As I showed in Chapter 4, companies will experiment continuously with different types of strategies, to which volunteers will respond differently depending on their perceived value and the needs of the software, and their trust in the firms.

My discussion of the dependencies that develop between firms and communities in FL/OSS development is guided by Foucault's views on the relational and productive character of power relations. The adoption of his ideas for the study of FL/OSS reveals that the interpenetration of social and economic relations is an inherently ambiguous process that creates different opportunities for agency and control among individuals, firms and communities. The findings on the challenges and opportunities that emerge as grassroots projects grow and consolidate their links with the market economy illustrate quite aptly how power relations become embedded within and disembedded from the social fabric of FL/OSS communities. They also reveal some important axes of relations of power in FL/OSS communities. These include the need to balance the requirements of access with the ability to be reliable about delivering a high-quality product and to accommodate a diversity of expertise within a predominantly technical community.

COMMERCIALIZATION AND THE ROLE OF EMPLOYED DEVELOPERS

The findings from the case studies of the GNOME and KDE communities (presented in Chapter 5) about how companies and communities align their interests confirm that grassroots FL/OSS communities take steps to accommodate, commercial requirements (O'Mahony, 2002). These steps include efforts to make more regular releases of new program versions and create organizational bodies entrusted to liaise between communities and commercial actors. In Chapter 5, I argued that this view is consistent with the idea of corporate players as clients, actors external to the community, whose needs are catered to through an organized response on the part of the community members. However, in examining the role of paid contributors in community-initiated and -led FL/OSS projects, it was revealed that relations between the spheres of the gift and the market economies are far more complex than this perspective might suggest. In particular, closer examination reveals a complex 'embedding' of firms in the space of FL/OSS projects, through the hiring of individuals with close community ties. The study of this group of contributors produced some very interesting findings on the role of firms and the implications of their involvement in grassroots FL/OSS projects.

Employed developers with close community ties, and especially those who previously worked as volunteers in a project, embody a network of connections and extensive know-how about community processes which facilitate acceptance of their work and collaboration with other community members. The analyses of the networks of members of KDE e.V. and the GNOME Foundation and these two projects' maintainer networks, confirmed the importance of the role played by this embedded expression of corporate presence in the development process. The results indicate that employed developers are involved in and maintain crucial infrastructural aspects of development and participate more regularly than volunteers in major community events. Based on this, I would argue again that, compared to volunteers, paid developers are in a better position to cultivate the knowledge and technical competence required to enable a substantial contribution to critical parts of the code base, because they can work on projects full-time and have the resources to enable regular attendance at community events.

In addition, employed developers appear to introduce an element of continuity into project life cycles. Many of the employed developers I interviewed were long-term contributors who were at the centre of development and community life. This is particularly important because FL/OSS development is characterized by high turnover of developers. Employed developers, therefore, would seem to play a significant role in maintaining a community memory, especially with regard to those aspects of development and community life that cannot be retrieved or easily reconstructed from a project's online records, such as the rationale for crucial policy or technical decisions.[3]

At the same time, many employed developers appear to be rather sensitive about balancing corporate and community interests. Their motivations may not coincide entirely with those of their employers. My study indicates that many of them are willing to assume responsibilities beyond their employment remit and to maintain parts of the code base on a volunteer basis. They also develop tactics for avoiding engagement in projects that they consider contradict the interests of communities. The interpenetration of professional relations with social relations and the importance of social norms can limit the influence of the firm on peer-established and institutionally independent FL/OSS projects. This suggests an interesting question for a follow-up study: whether the commitment of these individuals to community values is so strong that they would continue to work on FL/OSS projects even when no longer required to do so by their employers. However, the process of commercialization is not unproblematic. The case of GStreamer/Fluendo points to the difficulties involved in making the transition from a purely volunteer based project (Gstreamer) to one involving a corporate player (Fluendo SL). Fluendo employees feared that the faster rate of development could alienate volunteers who were unable to dedicate sufficient time to keep up to speed with the changes made to the code base by firm employees. In addition, the hiring of a number of key Gstreamer programmers by Fluendo SL blurred the distinction between company and community, making it difficult sometimes to question the firm's agenda.

How can different agendas and priorities be taken account of in the FL/OSS development process? The GNOME Bounty Hunt prompted a fascinating debate about the extent to which commercial requirements, Novell Inc.'s in this case, should be responded to. It also raised some interesting questions with regard to whether and how these types of initiatives bring in new contributors or whether they simply reallocate resources and reshuffle priorities within the community. The Bounty Hunt revealed that FL/OSS projects are not spaces of abundance, a main characteristic of the gift economy, but are instead sites where community resources are viewed as limited and requiring management. At the same time, the contest highlighted the complexity of defining and implementing a coherent and transparent development agenda and questioned how different voices and interests are represented within projects. The embedded character of FL/OSS development makes it difficult for some actors, who lack the skills or the willingness to engage in the development process, to satisfy their needs. Another reason why the idea of the contest was controversial was that it represented a clear market intervention that was not mediated by the social fabric of the community, as happens in the case of paid community members. As such it was seen as having the potential to tip the balance in favour of monetary incentives and undermine the volunteer basis of the GNOME project.

AUTONOMOUS PERIPHERALITY, LEARNING AND THE DIVISION OF LABOUR

There is an interesting dilemma common to both communities and companies: the need to cultivate and maintain a high level of technical excellence and to deliver a high-quality product on time. This demand may raise the barriers to access to the point where they discourage new volunteers from joining projects. After all, it is to the benefit of the company as much as to the community to retain the volunteer aspect of projects and to maintain the balance in favour of the gift economy. Many communities make attempts to lower the barriers to participation by producing documentation and tutorials or participating in initiatives, such as the Google Summer of Code, which introduce semi-formal mentoring arrangements.

The findings from the study of barriers to access for new contributors in the KDE and GNOME projects indicate that joining mature FL/OSS projects is not simply a process of enculturation, but is shaped by the pressure to deliver and is underpinned by significant obstacles. The study examines the issue of learning and integration from the perspectives of newbies—new developers and senior developers. The findings suggest that newbies face three types of difficulties: (i) familiarization with the tools of FL/OSS development; (ii) conceptual difficulties in understanding how organizational arrangements are structured and how specific processes are related to one another; and (iii) problems related to how individuals present and situate themselves in the development process, that is, what tasks they choose and how they ask for support. This last barrier may be associated with broader cultural issues of how individuals are accustomed to functioning in a learning environment and what expectations they have about guidance from senior people.

A crucial element in mobilizing help from senior developers in FL/OSS development is the demonstration of an understanding of the requirements of FL/OSS development from the earliest stages of the process of seeking assistance. Established members of the community prefer to support individuals who are able clearly to identify the tasks they want to undertake and who can demonstrate an understanding of the issues and processes involved. These expectations are related to two key characteristics of new contributors that senior developers value: self-reliance and commitment. The high turn-over of contributors and the significant demands made on the time of experienced developers seem to be the main factors shaping these expectations. In mature FL/OSS communities, therefore, legitimate peripheral participation is expected to be a solitary activity that takes place in the background rather than in the forefront of development.

A key finding emerging from the GNOME and KDE case studies is that learning relations in FL/OSS are embedded in a framework of cooperation shaped by the demands of continuous production, the decentralized and socially embedded character of collaboration, and the tensions between the collectivist and individualist aspects of participation. These factors shape a framework of participation in which independence, value and self-initiative are appreciated, and where the time and attention of senior developers must be earned. The process of learning is as much a process of enculturation as a process of integration into a professional network, a process of familiarization with a specific software methodology and code base. From this perspective, learning relations are relations of power: they are an integral part of processes that control access and participation.[4]

Community efforts to invite contributions from external developers, however, do not run contrary to senior developers' views that learning challenges are a (necessary) selection mechanism. In Chapter 6, I argued that efforts to lower the barriers to participation are especially important to encourage incremental contributions from developers who remain at the periphery of the FL/OSS community. The expectations of senior developers appear to be of concern to those developers who are able to make more substantial contributions and may eventually move to the centre of the community.[5]

There are, however, additional barriers to access. As in so many aspects of social life, race, gender, geography, language and culture underlie many power dynamics in FL/OSS development. According to a FL/OSS developer working for Sun Microsystems, the Indian programmers working for Wipro Ltd, who were used to more hierarchical modes of development and traditional apprenticeship relations than those applying in the context of community development, were often reluctant to take the initiative. A

Chilean developer I met at GUADEC admitted in conversation that many of his colleagues were reluctant to contribute to IRC channels because they were not confident about their English-language skills. The question of gender also is often an issue among FL/OSS developers, but it has never been examined systematically.

The investigation of non-programming contributions led to my phrase *autonomous peripherality* to encapsulate the unique characteristics and organization of non-programming activities within FL/OSS projects. I argue that autonomous peripherality is not simply a preparatory stage to joining the main programming community, but is a distinct sphere of activity. In contrast to programmers who focus on technical excellence and experimentation, non-programming contributors emphasize the values of access and ease of use. Analysis of the profiles of GNOME Foundation and KDE e.V. members indicates that autonomous peripheral contributors are predominantly volunteers. This is another factor that distinguishes the constellation of non-programming contributors from the core programming community which is strongly associated with paid contributors, especially at the level of maintainers.

The organization of autonomous peripheral teams indicates that contributions made by translators and documenters are seasonal: they intensify during freezes which are the periods preceding major releases when development is halted. This allows these teams to catch up with the progress made by the coding teams and to finalize their work. Accommodating the needs of translators and documenters requires a non-active phase of development and a willingness on the part of coders to resist tinkering with code prior to a release, and this may introduce tensions in the cooperation between coders and non-coding contributors. Although the value of non-coding contributors is being recognized increasingly, it is widely acknowledged that peripheral contributors are generally less likely than programmers to achieve high status within the community. The need to maintain a coherent community base that is welcoming to both non-programming contributors and newbies, but which does not alienate the technical part of the community, constitutes another axis in the power relations in FL/OSS.

Autonomous and legitimate peripheral participation are important because they reflect the challenges and tensions that emerge in FL/OSS projects as they grow and reach both non-technical audiences and more diverse and specialized communities of users. On the one hand, FL/OSS projects need to maintain the capacity to recruit new, capable members while balancing quality and access. On the other hand, FL/OSS communities need to integrate different types of expertise, including domain specific skills, without alienating the technical community. Although issues of usability and documentation are frequently part of the added value firms bring to FL/OSS, the significance of translation, accessibility and usability activities in the context of GNOME and KDE indicate that many contributors consider them to be crucial aspects of FL/OSS in promoting access by addressing the needs of minority groups that cannot be fulfilled by proprietary alternatives.

The picture that emerges from this part of the study highlights FL/OSS communities as constituted of constellations of practices, connected by the projects' overarching goals, but distinctive in terms of their priorities, development rhythms and patterns of collaboration. Although the significance and nature of autonomous peripherality depends on the knowledge domain of the projects and the particular types of users that they involve they are an understudied, but important, aspect of development that contributes greatly to the overall quality and user experience of a project.

TECHNOLOGIES OF COMMUNITIES: A NEW WAY OF ORGANIZING LABOUR RELATIONSHIPS

What can be said about the FL/OSS model of organization and cooperation in the light of this complex and diversified view of participation and collaboration? At the beginning of this book, I set out three principles that I consider to be fundamental for organizing and sustaining participation in FL/OSS projects. These are a programme of meritocracy, the invocation and enactment of community, and the tools and techniques for community management. These aspects of FL/OSS development represent the ways in which communities are constructed both as independent actors—that is, subjects of governance—and as objects—assets that can be managed— and the tools that they use to accomplish their purposes and retain and attract members.

These three principles are characterized as 'technologies of communities'. This concept extends Nikolas Rose's idea of 'technologies of communities', which is based on the Foucauldian definition of technology as a set of techniques and processes that cultivate certain skills and attitudes. Rose (1999: 189) uses the Foucauldian notion of technology to account for the increasing importance of communities as 'third spaces of action' in modern political discourse and considers technologies of communities to refer to the 'devices and techniques that make communities real'. Technologies of communities represent values, such the social basis of the organization of FL/OSS communities, whose potential cannot be realized in their purest form. Similar to the 'witches brew' that is the reality of life in prison compared to the pristine layout of the Panopticon,[6] the values, norms and processes represented by the different elements of technologies are articulated in a space that is permeated by competing interests and forces. They are still important, however. Analysis of the different elements of technologies of communities provides us with another lens for understanding the meaning and function of a widely accepted set of ideals, tools and processes that reveals the truth about the FL/OSS phenomenon—that of a redefinition of the relationship between sociality and economic production.

THE PROGRAMME OF MERITOCRACY

Why does meritocracy provide such an enduring explanation of the organization of FL/OSS projects? From the beginning of the book I have stressed how meritocracy is regarded as offering an equitable basis for participation and for establishing a hierarchy that emerges organically from the process of development. Equality of opportunity, however, does not confer equality of outcome. In Chapter 2, I referred to some of the factors that may influence an individual's progression through a project's hierarchy, explaining them in terms of the small-world character of many FL/OSS networks. In commercially-founded and -managed FL/OSS projects, the equitable character of participation can be even more skewed as firms will frequently retain control over the most important technical and policy decisions. It could also be argued that some contributors have more opportunities to excel than others. Native English speakers and developers who are hired to work full-time on FL/OSS projects are in better positions to make substantial contributions and, therefore, have more say in the development process. There is also the question of the definition of merit, of who defines it and of what it means specifically for the way power relations are articulated in FL/OSS development.

The reasons for the persistence of the meritocratic programme are multifaceted. First, the programme is very effective in establishing and sustaining a detailed system of differentiation that underpins the individualistic aspects of the hacker culture. This is expressed through multiple types of membership associated with a significant number of informal and formal groups with overlapping boundaries. Large FL/OSS communities are rife with technical and administrative committees, work groups organized on the basis of different activities and initiatives and, in some cases, mailing lists and IRC channels, access to which is subject to various vetting procedures. This landscape shapes different opportunities for inclusion and exclusion, which means that there is always something to achieve, something to learn and opportunities for individuals to distinguish themselves. This kind of visibility is a prerequisite for accruing reputational benefits, which can translate to better offers and access to venture capital (Lerner and Tirole, 2002; Roberts et al., 2006).

The definition of meritocracy as technocracy resonates with programmers' perceptions of the value of their work and the contributions made by other groups of employees in the workplace. Thus, programmers place a higher premium on their particular skills which are often framed in terms of a craft (Himanen, 2001). In addition, they consider their role as critical in terms of accountability, as they frequently constitute an obvious target for blame within organizations when there are failures or something does not function as it is supposed to do (Schaefer, 2006). Furthermore, as Tracy Kidder's (2000) account illustrates, developers often feel that their pursuit of excellence is constrained by organizational politics and the need to accommodate the demands of other groups such as clients and managers. At first glance, FL/OSS projects appear to provide an ideal space for developers to concentrate on their work unhindered by the politics of the workplace and the demands of other stakeholders. The persistence of technocracy is indicated by the shared perception that coding skills are definitely more valuable than other skills, and this is connected perhaps to the desire to maintain FL/OSS projects as pure, technical spaces.

The third function of meritocracy lies in its role in upholding the community's autonomy and openness which is essential for ensuring consensus and promoting recruitment. As my research has shown, community members accept the contributions of non-integrated, hired developers as long as they are subject to the same rigorous process of peer review that applies to volunteers. The case of paid developers with close community ties is more complicated. Although their affiliation is not a secret, they are often treated as if their employment does not really matter. For example, one interviewee indicated that on assuming a high organizational position, such as taking a place on the GNOME Board of Directors, hired programmers are not expected to represent anyone but themselves. It is possible that the reluctance to dispute the loyalty and merit of integrated paid developers stems from the need to protect the meritocratic basis of their participation.[7]

THE INVOCATION OF COMMUNITY

Whereas the first element of technologies of community concerns the programme of meritocracy where the basis and sources of authority are established for creating a socially grounded hierarchy, the second element of technologies of communities concerns the way in which the idea of community is employed and performed to mobilize resources and maintain a unified basis of participation. At the beginning of the book, I suggested that this strategy has ritualistic and strategic aspects: both personal and team performances are essential for sustaining the idea of a coherent community, while allowing actors to position themselves strategically in their efforts to mobilize volunteer resources.

As I have noted at several junctures, volunteer participation continues to form the backbone of FL/OSS projects. As an increasing number of volunteer contributors seek to make a living from their involvement in projects, and small and large companies attempt to reap the benefits of FL/OSS development, volunteer participation, arguably the most coveted resource of FL/OSS projects, can no longer be taken for granted. Most of those who are familiar with the dynamics of FL/OSS development understand that sustained exploitation requires sustained involvement through the grounding of contributors in the network of relations that permeate the community; continued reassurance that the community is a separate, autonomous space; and an understanding of how to appeal to common values in order to mobilize community resources.

For firm-initiated and -controlled FL/OSS projects, the credibility that is assigned to the invocation of the idea of community by firms is dependent on their trustworthiness and reputation as good citizens within the larger community of FL/OSS. In Chapter 4, I argued that firms aim to cultivate a consistent positive image by creating a network of credible commitments that might include patent pledges and transfers of software copyright to volunteer communities.

However, what is encompassed by the idea of community is not always self-evident. Does the notion of community, for example, include the user community alongside the developer, coder and peripheral communities? Does it include the social as well as the technical? As the case studies of the GNOME and KDE projects reveal, these communities overlap in terms of their overarching goals, but are, at the same time, quite distinctive in terms of their make up and priorities. In addition, access to different groupings and teams within projects is structured. Current discourses emphasize the importance of the developer community over the value of autonomous, peripheral, participant contributions. The invocation of the idea of a unified community across different sites—in spite of, or because of, its multiplicity—is therefore essential to establish and sustain it as an autonomous space.

The significance of the invocation of a unified community is reflected in the importance placed on the image of the community that is projected and the processes of control underlying different types of membership and forms of representation. Control over official representation of the community is strictly regulated within projects. For instance, modification rights for the GNOME and KDE websites are more difficult to obtain than access to the CVS. The existence of gated mailing lists can also be seen as an essential part of maintaining the integrity of 'front stage' performances in creating a separate backstage space where certain issues can be discussed more openly. In addition to the evolution of expressions of formal membership, such as recognition of the value of non-coding contributions, some supporting higher-level activities are becoming increasingly professionalized. In 2008, for example, the GNOME Board hired a director for business development.[8]

Invoking the idea of community, however, takes on an additional, strategic significance based on the way different groups are perceived and depicted and affect one another according to different contexts of interaction—that is, within more public or more private spaces. One of the individuals primarily responsible for the GNOME Bounty Hunt, for instance, suggested that the contest, among other things, enabled users to get closer to developers. This suggestion contradicts the established view of a direct relationship between users and programmers and highlights how the different perceptions of users and their needs can be mobilized as part of a specific agenda.

The connection of this technology with the programme of meritocracy lies in the need to maintain the primacy of the developer community while, at the same time, not alienating the peripheral community. In part, this can be achieved through the provision of a framework of access and representation which is based on the definition of meritocracy as technocracy, but which does not preclude non-programmers outright and provides preferential access for coders.

TOOLS AND TECHNIQUES FOR COMMUNITY MANAGEMENT

The third element of technologies of communities concerns the tools and techniques developed to address the problems of governance and management. The meaning and function of these tools and techniques is ambiguous. On the one hand, they are integral to the construction of FL/OSS as autonomous spaces, as subjects of governance. On the other hand, they form an important part of the strategies of actors who want to appropriate the benefits of FL/OSS. This element of technologies of communities does not include specific governance or management models, but involves the lower-level tools and techniques that are required for their exercise. This aspect of technologies of communities is associated with the emergence of a body of knowledge focusing on the constitution and management of communities, not only in FL/OSS, but also in politics, science and the workplace.

Although not always framed in political terms (Coleman, 2004), the balances between openness and control, coordination and decentralization, political power, legal representation and technical authority are continuously debated and reflected upon in FL/OSS projects. The issues of governance and management and their models, principles and mechanisms are inextricably related to efforts to survey, map and visualize community space (Rose, 1999). As shown in Chapter 3, FL/OSS activity generates a flood of data that includes various types of documentation; mail and CVS digests (reports of code contributions made to the CVS repositories); personalized individual, module and bug statistics; websites that aggregate feeds from developer blogs (like Planet GNOME); and a complicated network of websites. Given the fluid nature of FL/OSS communities, it is certainly true that in the absence of these data it would be impossible to identify what needs to be managed, governed or represented. The generation and use of these data, therefore, are prerequisites for visualizing and organizing the development process; surveying and mapping participant networks in all their different expressions (social, technical, etc.); and measuring performance and authenticating participation.

The wide availability of data generated through the development process provides opportunities for action and intervention on both the individual and collective levels. Data relating to code contributions obtained through CVS, for example, allow leading developers to make critical decisions regarding when the software is ready to be released. Reports on program defects obtained through bug databases enable programmers to pinpoint critical faults and areas requiring more work. Data related to individuals' contributions, in principle, can be used to authenticate participation and to evaluate performance which is crucial for situating them in a project meritocratic hierarchy. Lastly, the use of aggregated blog feeds and the development of tools such as maps depicting the location of contributors across the globe can assist in visualization of participant networks and their overlapping social and technical expression.

A recurrent challenge in FL/OSS development is to manage the activities and delivery times of globally distributed volunteers over whom little control can be exercised. The lessons learned, both individually and collectively, inform new techniques for managing them. Time-based release, as we have seen, is an important coordination mechanism, and developers have been developing innovative tactics for time management. A high-level KDE programmer, for example, described how the publication of the release schedule, together with the incremental freezes and the accompanying announcements at each stage of the process, were utilized to get people into that 'freeze feeling' to develop a sense of urgency in the light of a looming deadline (Roger, 22.08.04).

At the same time, the knowledge generated through engagement in the FL/OSS development process is increasingly formalized and commoditized. In an address to the Massachusetts Software Council titled 'The Mechanics of Open Source: Growing and Harvesting your Open Source Project', Nat Friedman and Miguel de Icaza (2005), the founders of GNOME, described some of the basic requirements for a successful FL/OSS project. These included the need to maintain a core working group and the benefit of providing concrete tasks for people to become involved in. Friedman and de Icaza utilized the insights they gleaned from development in the GNOME project to set up the MONO platform, another FL/OSS project controlled by Novell Inc., which provides a FL/OSS implementation of Microsoft's .Net architecture.

This migration of knowledge acquired in the context of FL/OSS development, combined with the perceived benefits of FL/OSS for commercial purposes, has given rise to a body of knowledge related to the constitution and management of volunteer FL/OSS communities (Goldman and Gabriel, 2005; Haruvy et al., 2003; West and O'Mahony, 2008). The continuing popularity of studies on developers' motivations is indicative of the effort to understand and, to some extent, control participation. As FL/OSS software is increasingly regarded as a potential engine for innovation and development, connecting and cultivating FL/OSS communities becomes a priority for transnational, national and regional institutions. The significance of the role of FL/OSS communities as new spaces of innovation and production reflects parallel developments regarding the perceived importance of communities in areas as diverse as science, politics and the workplace (Cross and Parker, 2004; Knorr-Cetina, 1999) and the emergence of a body of knowledge geared towards their cultivation and management (Wenger et al., 2002).

Table 7.1 presents the main elements of technologies of communities, the strategies and tools and tactics that constitute them, and their function within the context of FL/OSS communities

Table 7.1 Summary of the Main Characteristics and Functions of Technologies of Communities

Technologies of communities	Function (what)	Tools, techniques (how)	Result
The programme of meritocracy	Definition of meritocracy as technocracy	Assigning different values to different contributions, maintaining primacy of coding skills	Establishing a socially grounded hierarchy of participation and access
	Maintaining a detailed system of differentiations through the creation of different types of membership	Creating opportunities and motives for excellence (individualistic aspect of the hacker culture)	
	Promoting recruitment and maintaining participation	Upholding the community's autonomy and openness, protection against distorting effects of commercialization and formal organization	
The invocation of community	Appeal to common values (ritual invocation)	Importance placed on the image of the community, sustaining 'front stage' performances	Establishing community as a unified, positive space
	Tactics for mobilising volunteer resources (strategic invocation)	Ways in which different groups are perceived and depicted	
Tools and techniques for community management	Surveying, mapping community space and performance of contributors	Generation and use of data related to the development process at the individual and community level	Establishing community as a subject and object of governance
	Managing globally distributed labour	Modularity, time based releases, use of scheduling to incentivize participation	
	Emergence of a body of knowledge related to managing communities	Formalization of practitioners' knowledge, related research	

Although they are distinctive, the technologies of communities are interconnected. The tools for surveying and mapping community space are essential both for the fulfilment of the programme of meritocracy and for the tactics required for managing development and the people that are employed to mobilize volunteer resources. At the same time, the establishment of community as a subject and object of governance presupposes its establishment as an autonomous space.

The interweaving of these technologies of communities with project-specific characteristics and dynamics, including those established through their 'architecture of participation',[9] creates different opportunities for alignment and control between the participants in the development process. In the case of communities that are independent from companies, the tools that enable the survey of community space can be employed by community members who want to pinpoint and address development bottlenecks, as well as by companies interested in appropriating parts of the code base or by those scouting for potential employees. In the case of communities that feature groups of non-coding contributors, the appeal to common values and ideas helps to mobilize the contributions of non-programmers, whose work is usually seen as less worthy than that of coders. It also adds to the perception of community as a unified space. This unity is undermined when the priorities and agendas of different groups of contributors are taken into account. Can the idea of technologies of communities apply to corporately initiated and controlled FL/OSS projects? I think that the deciding factors in this case are the meanings that contributors assign to the idea of community and the values that they derive from their participation, on the one hand, and on the way that corporate actors handle the dynamics between access and control, on the other. In cases where FL/OSS is used as a distribution mechanism (see Chapter 4), invoking the idea of community is unimportant. If, however, the mobilization of volunteer contributions is deemed to be critical, but is far from certain, then we would expect that the different elements of technologies of communities would come into play.

THE MORAL ECONOMY: THE ASYMMETRIES BETWEEN THE GIFT AND THE MARKET ECONOMIES

Foucault conceived power as an inherently productive force (1979). Unlike predominant views of power that focus on its repressive, negative and institutional aspects, Foucault's relational approach to power emphasizes its capacity to shape and direct knowledge and is intended to highlight its often unintended and ambiguous results. The approach that I have adopted here uses this perspective to highlight the opportunities and tensions that emerge through the continuing transformation of FL/OSS and its transformative potential to merge social and economic relations in new ways. These opportunities and tensions are shaped by the interweaving of technologies of communities, tools and ways of thinking, and action that constitute

FL/OSS communities as objects and subjects of governance with project specific characteristics and dynamics.

It is useful to consider the observations of this chapter in the light of Linus Torvalds's[10] comments in an interview that:

> the commercial concerns from the very beginning, even when they were small, were really very important. The commercial distributions were what drove a lot of the nice installers, and pushed people to improve usability etcetera, and I think commercial users of Linux have been very important in actually improving the product. I think all the technical people who have been involved have been hugely important, but I think that the kind of commercial use that you can get with the GPLv2 is also important—you need a balance between pure technology, and the kinds of pressures you get from users through the market.
>
> So I don't think marketing can drive that particular thing: if you have a purely marketing (or customer) driven approach, you end up with crap technology in the end. But I think that something that is purely driven by technical people will also end up as crap technology in the end, and you really need a balance here. So a lot of the really rabid 'Free Software' people seem to often think that it's all about the developers, and that commercial interests are evil. I think that's just stupid. It's not just about the individual developers; it's about all the different kinds of interests all being able to work on things together.

A potential explanation for the continuing transformation of FL/OSS is that the evolution of FL/OSS projects is following a similar trajectory to the evolution of the Internet and the development of other historical large-scale infrastructures (Braudel, 1982). This trajectory is characterized by a shift from the largely elitist bases of such systems to utilization by a wider population through the persistence of existing socio-economic structures. This transformation raises questions about whether FL/OSS software's supportive activities will continue to take place within the context of technical projects. Autonomous peripherality may develop its own, separate infrastructures similar to what occurred in the Open Usability project (see Chapter 5). Also, the transformation of FL/OSS involves an evolution in the way that different user groups are represented within projects. Despite the dominant view of the relationship between developers and users as being one of direct communication and feedback, my findings suggest that there are larger forces at play in formulating the development agendas of projects. User needs are generally represented either by corporate actors or by contributors who are interested in usability and accessibility—in other words, the end users' interests are often mediated.

Throughout the discussion of the role of companies in FL/OSS, I have emphasized the assignment of FL/OSS roles to employees and the hiring of individuals from the ranks of volunteer contributors. One of the reasons why companies with interests in FL/OSS projects prefer to hire volunteer contributors formally is that this allows them to integrate their corporate agendas into the community-development process. However, the hiring of these volunteers affects the company's organizational culture and processes. When asked about the challenges involved in reconciling company and community needs, a KDE developer argued that 'we have changed SUSE more than SUSE has changed us' (Dean, 22.03.04). This feeling of empowerment is usually reflected in the role(s) that paid developers assume within the context of their organizations and the tactics they employ to keep their professional and community involvement aligned (see Chapter 4). In large organizations with less prominent FL/OSS agendas, these individuals often assume the roles of educators of and/or mediators between the community and the corporate teams that are unfamiliar with FL/OSS processes.

Examination of the network of companies supporting members of the KDE e.V. and the GNOME Foundation and the two communities' maintainer networks (Chapters 4 and 5) revealed the nature of the business environment that is developing as a result of the commercial appropriation. Although this environment includes some large players, it is mainly characterized by a substantial number of small, medium and even microenterprises (built around one or two developers) and public institutions. Although further research and a more systematic examination are needed to investigate more fully the relations developing between these actors and their ties with FL/OSS, the current findings provide evidence of the work and entrepreneurship opportunities FL/OSS offers to individuals situated between the gift and exchange economies.

At the end of the discussion of corporate strategies for appropriating FL/OSS (Chapter 4), I questioned whether it is possible to have an ethical FL/OSS business. An interesting idea that has been developed to characterize an equitable, ethical balance between the demands of the market economy and the dynamics of the gift economy is that of the 'moral economy' (Green and Jenkins, 2008; Jenkins et al., 2009). Borrowing the term from the British historian E. P. Thompson (1971), Green and Jenkins (2008) define the moral economy as the 'social expectations, emotional investments, and cultural transactions which create a shared understanding between all participants within an economic exchange'.[11] Another definition is provided by Edward Cheal (1988: 15), who argues that the moral economy 'is a system of transactions which are defined as socially desirable (i.e. moral), because through them social ties are recognized, and balanced social relationships are maintained'.

In evaluating the opportunities that emerge in this moral space for communities, firms and individuals, it is important to take into account the asymmetries in their abilities to position themselves in ways that best serve their interests. Although it is true that firms need to accommodate volunteer requirements, either in the context of their own FL/OSS projects or as participants in others, they are also in a better position to plan their actions strategically. In the context of the projects that they initiate they can set up the rules of the game and experiment with different configurations of control and openness. In the context of projects over which they have no formal control, they can influence the direction of development by hiring individuals who are advantageously placed in the community network. The hands-off approach of many community-led projects with regard to policy formulation makes them particularly vulnerable to such organized interventions. Is this perhaps one of the limits to the emergent social organization of grassroots FL/OSS projects, or is it an opportunity for FL/OSS communities to extend their horizons and rethink the way that they operate at a policy level? My thoughts on this issue are presented in the next and final chapter, Chapter 8.

8 Conclusions

I have discussed the evolving relationship between the gift and market economies by depicting the features of two spheres of activity. In the first, which I see as populated by commercial FL/OSS initiatives, control over how FL/OSS is used and developed rests primarily with firms. In the second sphere, which I see as constituted by communities that are founded and managed independently of firms, authority is distributed among contributors, and the directions of projects are defined by those who demonstrate the capacity to effect the most progress. By studying how these spheres merge—based in the first instance on the need to cultivate communities of external contributors, and in the second instance on the commercialization of grassroots FL/OSS projects—I have sought to illustrate hybridity, the blending of the gift and the market economies in their variegated forms.

The first question is whether, in becoming more deeply embedded in the dominant market flows, FL/OSS communities and especially grassroots communities can retain their independence from commercial interests and continue to develop a public good. I find that the answer is that the relationship between the gift and the market economies is ambiguous and asymmetrical. Within the context of grassroots projects that the sustained appropriation of volunteer labour can be achieved only through the cultivation of social relations, which, to an extent, serves to limit commercial influences. The complex embedding of firms in development processes through the hiring of contributors influences the dynamics of collaboration and has a major impact on the social organization of FL/OSS projects. The top-down control that characterizes firms as institutions enables the more efficient formulation and pursuit of strategies than is achievable in bottom-up collectives. Asymmetries in the relationship between the market and the gift economies are based largely on this differential in the ability to design and pursue strategies over time or in response to changing market conditions. The second key question addressed in this book concerns how FL/OSS transforms existing institutions: the answer to this is that at a strategic level firms select which elements of FL/OSS are best suited to their plans. They may adopt the methods and processes of FL/OSS development, but not necessarily its values. Their tactics are constrained by the social basis of FL/OSS development and by the fact that the most coveted resource of FL/OSS development, volunteer labour, is beyond their immediate control.

The picture that emerges from my study of FL/OSS development is one of diversity. The macro-level view of FL/OSS that I adopted in Chapters 3 and 4 reveals that the landscape of FL/OSS production is populated by a diverse collection of communities that coalesce in complex ways around FL/OSS projects. I highlighted the elements of the FL/OSS model of organization that are adopted in different contexts and the business strategies that exploit FL/OSS. The micro-level view in Chapters 5 and 6, in contrast, highlights how the adoption of FL/OSS affects the software development process and the division of labour in developer communities. In aligning their particular strategies and pursuing their particular interests, firms, individuals and communities are experimenting with various approaches with varying degrees of success.

However, there appear to be regularities with regard to the strategies that have proven successful in the context of peer production. Invocation of the idea of community, for example, needs to be founded on trust relations, an understanding that talk about shared values and aims is not a public relations exercise, but rather is founded on real commitment and the desire to support the collective effort. The conditions needed to mobilize and organize volunteers effectively, highlight the fundamental elements of commons-based peer production which I term 'technologies of communities'. In this final chapter, I draw out the broader implications of the observations in this book with respect to the reconfiguration of the relations between sociality and economic production that FL/OSS embodies.

OPEN-ENDED FIRMS AND CONSTELLATIONS OF COMMUNITIES

FL/OSS software is a valuable commodity. It is valuable because it provides an alternative to proprietary solutions and because its unique characteristics enable users to adapt it to requirements and needs not provided for by the market. I have discussed the commitment of the contributors who translate FL/OSS programs into many different languages and who focus on improving software accessibility for impaired individuals. FL/OSS, as a social and economic form of organization, is deeply connected to issues of access and development. It has value also because it can be used to generate revenues. I have directed attention to the business models that have evolved around grassroots FL/OSS projects, including those of self-employed FL/OSS contributors, and discussed the conditions under which firms usually release proprietary software under a FL/OSS licence. Of equal value to FL/OSS as a commodity is the creative energy and productivity of FL/OSS contributors. The ideas and improvements constantly generated through the process of FL/OSS development by dozens—sometimes hundreds—of volunteers, and the opportunities for learning that arise through collaboration, motivate firms to participate in FL/OSS development and to cultivate their own technical communities.

FL/OSS business practices and the growing dependency of firms on volunteer labour appear to promise change in the way that firms conduct their business, and in their culture. Many employed FL/OSS practitioners would seem to agree, suggesting that their presence and the requirements of FL/OSS development, force employers and colleagues to revise established business ideas and ingrained approaches to software development. This tends to echo the claims of proponents of 'open' and 'user innovation', who argue that firms have much to gain from opening up their boundaries and adjusting their processes better to utilize input from external contributors (Chesbrough, 2006; von Hippel, 2007). However, the reality in FL/OSS is different. Rather than relinquishing control, firms involved in FL/OSS often simply transpose it. There is evidence that firms are likely to release software under an established FL/OSS licence when they are well positioned to control important complementary assets and have developed expertise around these assets that is difficult to replicate (Fosfuri et al., 2008). Firms are also more likely to retain ownership over the code that they release under a FL/OSS licence and to maintain tight control over the production process (see Chapter 4). In order to engage volunteers in their projects successfully, however, firms need to demonstrate a capacity to serve as the trustees of a collective effort. This frequently involves forging a network of commitments. Many of these, such as patent pledges, are expressions merely of goodwill rather than binding agreements. The extent to which firms' commitments and strategies will persist following a buyout by another firm, or an important shift in market conditions, is always uncertain. During the five years that I was studying FL/OSS, many insurgent firms that emerged to commercialize FL/OSS was bought up by larger firms. It would be interesting to examine how this change repositions these insurgents in terms of their relations and commitments to the FL/OSS community.

A more radical shift towards more-open business approaches emerges when firms become involved in FL/OSS projects that are beyond the immediate control of the single firm. In this case, firms embed themselves by hiring developers with established community ties or by encouraging their staff to develop such ties with FL/OSS developments. In this context, the interpenetration of social and economic relations has important implications for communities as well as firms. The mediation of employment relations through the social fabric of the community, limits commercial influence to some extent. The more established a FL/OSS community, and the greater the number of firms participating in the development process, the less likely it is that a single company will capture the software development agenda. The actions and motivations of employed developers are less likely to reflect the agendas and desires of their employers in their entirety. Also, many employed developers with close community ties take on tasks beyond what their employers expect. I also encountered individuals who admitted to avoiding completing work that they considered would run counter to community interests. However, the hands-off approach of many FL/OSS communities with respect to how their development agendas evolve, renders such plans vulnerable to the effects of decisions by firms that may effect substantial changes in the direction of projects. My findings on the composition of the GNOME and KDE maintainers' networks suggest that many employed developers maintain key infrastructural parts of the code base, which means that such changes are likely to be adopted. Although the involvement of firms with different agendas may help to (re) establish plurality within the context of FL/OSS communities, this is not an inevitable outcome. Firms are institutions of capitalism that are designed to act and plan strategically: grassroots FL/OSS communities are not designed similarly. These communities need to develop governance processes that will allow them to consult, decide and enforce the policies they want to pursue. Emergent community structures, such as the GNOME Foundation and KDE e.V., currently do not have such decision-making processes in place. This issue is not easily addressed, not because of a lack of interest, but rather because of the potentially disruptive character and high cost that coordination might involve. These types of interventions could be seen as contradicting the meritocratic basis of participation at another fundamental level (Coleman, 2005) by creating an elite, bureaucratic class that undermines the emergent social organization of FL/OSS development.

In terms of the social basis of the FL/OSS development process, the fact that many actions and decisions have to be mediated through the social fabric of the community is not always a positive force. The need to cultivate social ties by acquaintance with the informal aspects of a community, getting to know who is responsible for what and who is more likely to respond positively to requests, require effort and dedication. This is one of the barriers that new developers are faced with when seeking help and attempting to situate themselves in the development process. The 'dark side' of the social organization of FL/OSS is visible also in relation to the GNOME Bounty Hunt, which raises questions about how the development agendas of FL/OSS projects are defined and whether it is legitimate to use monetary incentives to develop particular features. The Bounty Hunt and similar monetary incentives appear to undermine the authority of maintainers over the direction of their modules. Although this particular contest might have been organized better, a bid system does provide the means for individuals and organizations that lack the skills or willingness to contribute to the FL/OSS development process to have their aspirations considered and to establish or safeguard plurality in the development process.

The snapshot of the division of labour in the GNOME and KDE projects that I provided in Chapters 5 and 6 indicates that an analysis of the embedded and emergent character of the social organization of grassroots FL/OSS projects yields a spatial model in which the centre—the stable core of the community—comprises mainly paid developers and the periphery mainly volunteers. The periphery provides the extra labour essential for the operation of the gift economy. I stressed the importance of autonomous peripheral participation in the aspects of documentation, accessibility, translation and usability that complement the technical aspects of development and improve the overall quality of the software. Recognition of autonomous peripherality as a distinct sphere of activity, rather than as a set of routine tasks that new developers need to perform as part of their apprenticeship, requires us to rethink existing approaches to the division of labour in FL/OSS that focus only on programming tasks. The importance and awareness of these activities and the groups and individuals that undertake them is not generally acknowledged, although within FL/OSS communities, as illustrated by my study of the GNOME and KDE projects, there is a wider recognition of the value of these contributions. Autonomous peripherality is essential because it is linked intrinsically to the importance of FL/OSS for addressing the requirements of those that are underserved by markets and who, as a consequence, are deprived of the benefits and opportunities offered by increased connectivity. FL/OSS cannot fulfil this important role unless these needs are expressed and represented in the FL/OSS development process.

TECHNOLOGIES OF COMMUNITIES AND THE MORAL ECONOMY

The story of FL/OSS that I have provided highlights the variety of experience and tactics that emerge in a space where the relations between sociality and economic production are being articulated in new ways. I have highlighted the dynamics of the forces that give rise to such variety and some of the tensions at the heart of FL/OSS as an agent of social and economic change. The unique character of FL/OSS production lies in the convergence of ideas, values and processes that allow communities to be established as subjects and objects of governance, capable of governing themselves and of being governed by others, which I describe as technologies of communities. This insight allows us to peel back the meaning in some widely accepted ideas and practices related to FL/OSS, to highlight how they organize and sustain collaboration. The first element of technologies of communities, the programme of meritocracy, refers to the sources and bases of authority within projects. Although, in practice, equality of opportunity does not confer equality of outcome, the assumption that the most active and capable contributors also have the greatest power to shape the direction of FL/OSS projects is an essential aspect of the received understanding of the social stratification of FL/OSS communities. I have suggested that the increased adoption of FL/OSS calls into question the view of FL/OSS projects as purely spaces of technical innovation: they are also spaces of complementary skills and expertise. The growth of FL/OSS projects also highlights the negative implications of the embedded character of FL/OSS development. The question of how merit and value are defined and verified plays an increasingly important role in peer production, as illustrated by socially produced reputation scoring (e.g., Amazon's and eBay's feedback systems), which is rapidly becoming one of the most important forms of social production (Strahilevitz, 2007).

The second element of technologies of communities, the invocation of the idea of community, concerns the way in which this notion is used and enacted to mobilize resources and to maintain a unified basis of participation in FL/OSS. This is necessary as the meaning of community is not always evident. The character of FL/OSS communities as constellations of practice invites us to consider their heterogeneity and the groups and individuals that populate them. In addition to understanding their integrative aspects, which enable a synthesis of diverse contributions, it is essential to consider how groups and interests are represented, whose voices are heard, and what voice the community assumes, collectively, through its representation. Exploring these aspects of communities in other areas of peer production would provide a basis for comparing the experience of FL/OSS with, for example, crowdsourcing. We need to develop new vocabularies to describe these emergent types of community and the different forms of sociality and reprocity that are evolving across the many contexts of peer production.

The third element of technologies of communities concerns the tools and techniques for community management. Similar to the other elements, the implications of the tools, tactics and processes for managing production are ambiguous. Analysis of the data generated by the FL/OSS development process would help FL/OSS communities to highlight potential bottlenecks and to prioritize the allocation of resources, but it could also encroach upon the privacy of contributors and be used for commercial purposes. Also important is the degree to which knowledge derived from the FL/OSS development process is formalized. There is a growing interest in how the creative energy of peer production could be channelled for commercial purposes. Nigel Thrift (2006) argues that the fascination with communities as drivers of innovation is the expression of a new trend in the capitalist model of commodification. The framework developed in this book takes account of the opportunities for agency offered by peer production, to individuals who wish to contribute to and benefit from the creation of a public good and the challenges created by the increased adoption of FL/OSS. In addition to the many other benefits of FL/OSS, these opportunities should include the ability both to make a livelihood and to pursue something about which one feels passionate. The development of a shared understanding with regard to what constitutes an ethical and equitable transaction system should not deny the importance of (at least modest) wealth. Peer production cannot function without individuals who can afford to commit themselves to the process full time. Sometimes this involves employment, the creation of a business or being rewarded for addressing specific problems. A moral economy is not simply about what limits are placed on how economic motivations encroach upon other social motivations, but about what kind of motives guide the process and outcome. It is about developing an understanding of how the wealth and the opportunities created through the process of peer production can be employed to address the limits of markets and promote the values of mutual empowerment.

Notes

NOTES TO CHAPTER 1

1. Source code refers to the set of instructions that make up a software program which can be read and understood by programmers. Proprietary software is distributed only in the form of object code, the machine-readable translation of the source code, which is required for computers to run programs and which is meaningful only to machines. Open source software is distributed as both source and object code.
2. These include von Hippel's (2007) ideas on user innovation and Chesbrough's (2006) views on open innovation.
3. GNU (pronounced gnu) is a recursive acronym that stands for 'GNU is not Unix'. It refers to the clone of the Unix operating system created by Richard Stallman.
4. VCSs are software tools that allow users to keep track of multiple versions of software under development.

NOTES TO CHAPTER 2

1. The term was first used by Karl Polanyi (1962) to describe a 'scientific commons' that is characterized by an open, democratic structure which permits the pursuit of scientific enquiry unconstrained by the demands of markets.
2. In the new institutional economics (Coase, 1937; Williamson, 1987), markets and firms are considered the principal institutional templates for the organization and coordination of the production of goods and services. Very simply put, firms rely on hierarchical, managerial control and can be conceptualized as clusters of resources and agents. They emerge as a distinctive organizational form, because under certain conditions they appear to coordinate production more efficiently than markets, where resources are allocated through the mechanism of price.
3. It has been argued that the same characteristics (the creation of common vocabularies, shared practices and bonds of trust) that allow information to be exchanged quickly within CoP may hinder information flows across their boundaries (Brown and Duguid, 2001; Duguid, 2003).
4. The idea was first expressed by Karl Polanyi (1944).
5. This idea of performance is based on the work of the sociologist, Erving Goffman (1969). Goffman defines the positive social values a person or a group effectively claims for itself through its individual or collective stance during particular social encounters, as a special type of performance called 'face-work'.

The concept of face-work is linked to a perceived positive social image that individuals and teams try to maintain.

6. In theoretical terms, I am interpreting the CoP perspective on the basis of a Foucauldian view of power.

NOTES TO CHAPTER 3

1. SourceForge (http://sourceforge.net/) is an online source code repository. It provides free hosting services and development tools to programmers interested in launching a FL/OSS project. It also serves as a directory for those who wish to search for and download a FL/OSS program and as a marketplace for those interested in obtaining support for FL/OSS products and services. It is said to include more than 230,000 registered projects as of February 2009 (http://apps.sourceforge.net/trac/sourceforge/wiki/What%20is%20SourceForge.net? last accessed 10.05.2009). Other major source code repositories are GNU Savannah (http://savannah.gnu.org/) and JavaForge for programs based on the Java programming language (http://javaforge.com).

2. In grassroots community projects, this virtuous cycle is established when the quality of the project is high enough to attract even more volunteers and where the cumulative impact of the number of the smallest contributions starts making a real difference in the development process.

3. For an overview of the motivations in FL/OSS communities, see David and Shapiro (2008) and Krishnamurthy (2006).

4. See http://www.debian.org/social_contract, last accessed 05.10.2008.

5. For workshop details, see http://msr.uwaterloo.ca/msr2009/index.html, last accessed 10.11.2009.

6. Copyright assignment involves the transfer of author copyright to a third party which may be the FL/OSS project to which they are contributing, an organization such as the FSF, or the company that is sponsoring the project. One reason why this is done is to centralize and enable copyright management. For more information see Chapter 4 in this book and http://www.softwarefreedom.org/resources/2008/foss-primer.html#x1-110002.3, last accessed 22.09.2008.

7. A CVS is an open source version or revision control software tool that allows developers to keep track of the changes in the code and to coordinate their work.

8. See Linux Kernel Mailing list FAQ at http://www.kernel.org/pub/linux/docs/lkml/#s3-7, last accessed 27.09.2008.

9. See Chapter 6 for an analysis of the importance of learning resources for new FL/OSS developers.

10. Robert Love is a senior engineer at Google who is well known for his work on the Linux Kernel. He has written a number of books with popular appeal on Linux kernel development.

11. Examples of these tools are provided in the wiki page maintained by the research team at http://tools.libresoft.es/, last accessed 05.10.2008.

12. Here, 'restrictive' refers to software licences requiring that any derivative works comply with the terms in the original. Many copyleft licences, such as GPL, are restrictive in character. Commercial licences are also restrictive. 'Permissive' licences—e.g. Berkeley Software Distribution and MIT licences—allow for more flexibility in the distribution of source code and derivative works, and the commingling of closed and open source code.

13. The sample was created by excluding from the population of projects hosted on SourceForge all those with fewer than 7 developers and fewer than 100 listed bugs.

14. The project is funded partly by the European Commission under Framework Programme 6, see http://www.sqo-oss.eu/, last accessed 15.10. 2008.
15. See http://www.openbrr.org/wiki/index.php/Home, last accessed 15.10.2008.
16. See, e.g., http://apps.sourceforge.net/trac/sitelegal/wiki/Crawler%20policy, last accessed 15.05.2009.
17. http://www.nd.edu/~oss/Data/data.html, last accessed 10.11.2008.
18. E.g., in the GNOME Foundation, what constitutes a substantial contribution—the basis for membership has evolved to include non-programming contributions.
19. Matthias Hasselman, blog entry, December 2007. See http://taschenorakel. de/mathias/2007/12/22/no-privacy-foss-developers/#c187, last accessed 11.11.2008.
20. See http://code.google.com/p/hackystat/, last accessed 18.11.2008.
21. Benjamin Mako Hill is on the Board of Directors of the FSF and is a long-term contributor to the Debian and Wikipedia projects.

NOTES TO CHAPTER 4

1. In 2007, Open Source Development Labs, whose mission was to accelerate Linux deployment in the business enterprise community, merged with the Free Standards Group to form the Linux Consortium.
2. Software Freedom Law Center home page at http://www.softwarefreedom. org/, last accessed 15.01.2009.
3. HP news release available at http://www.hp.com/hpinfo/newsroom/ press/2008/080124a.html, last accessed 15.01.2009.
4. An OSI approved licence is a FL/OSS licence that has been vetted through the OSI's licence-approval process and has been found to conform to the requirements and expectations regarding the terms of the redistributed of software as encapsulated by the Open Source Definition.
5. See press release at http://www-03.ibm.com/industries/education/us/detail/ news/M995153D19350W32.html, last accessed 02.01.2008.
6. In 2005 the Open Source Development Labs (part of the Linux Foundation) launched the Patent Commons Project (http://www.patentcommons.org/, last accessed 02.01.2008) a reference library of patent pledges made to the FL/OSS community.
7. See, e.g., http://www.pubpat.org/PUBPAT_Ltr_re_Sun_Patent_Grant.pdf, last accessed 9.05.2009.
8. The term 'synthetic' community was coined by West and O'Mahony (2008).
9. Discussions with GNOME and KDE e.V. showed that their perceptions of membership in these two organizations were different. Joining the GNOME Foundation appears to be regarded as an extension of one's identity as a community member, whereas participation in KDE e.V. is framed in narrower terms.
10. In Unix, the default interface, the means by which users communicate with the operating system, is provided by the shell, a command line interpreter. In a Microsoft windows-type desktop environment, users manage their computer, navigate the file system and launch applications by opening windows and clicking on icons, whereas in a shell environment users express commands by typing in directions, in a specific format. Although GUIs are easier to use, command-line interfaces offer users more control, speed and flexibility over the tasks they want to perform. Unix systems allow users to exploit both interfaces; experienced users switch seamlessly between the two.
11. In computing, a stack is a collection of systems or components designed to deliver a complete product or service. A stack implies that data and program

instructions are intermingled in the 'input' stream to a processor, and the syntax determines how this input stream is interpreted including whether it is accessed sequentially or in some other order.

12. See http://news.cnet.com/Nokia-debuts-Linux-based-Web-device/2100–1041_3–5720066.html, last accessed 15.01.2009.
13. A codec is a program that encodes or decodes digital streams of data.
14. See http://developers.slashdot.org/article.pl?sid=08/04/16/2337224, last accessed 02.01.2009.
15. See http://blogs.mysql.com/kaj/2008/05/06/mysql-server-is-open-source-even-backup-extensions/, last accessed 04.01.2009.
16. See http://gigaom.com/2008/03/30/the-gigaom-show-episode35-sun-ceo-jonathan-schwartz-show-is-taking-a-break/, last accessed 18.01.2009.
17. This was illustrated in the case of the relicensing of Mozilla; see http://www.mozilla.org/MPL/relicensing-faq.html#why-relicensing, last accessed 22.02.2009.
18. For an early discussion of this issue, see http://www.crynwr.com/cgi-bin/ezmlm-cgi?iis:8050:200209#b, last accessed 22.02.2009.

NOTES TO CHAPTER 5

1. In Veblen's (1921: 18) words, 'The cares of business have required an increasingly undivided attention on the part of the business men, and in an ever increasing measure their day's work has come to center about a running adjustment of sabotage on production'.
2. For more information see: http://live.gnome.org/ReleasePlanning/Time-Based, last accessed 02.02.2009.
3. See http://ldn.linuxfoundation.org/book/35-getting-official-buy-in and http://www.linuxfoundation.org/en/NDA_program, last accessed 2.02.2009.
4. The main concern here was that the kernel work concerned a product whose release the companies wished to keep secret.
5. In order to preserve anonymity, interviewees have been given aliases. The date refers to the date of the interview.
6. See http://nat.org/2005/january/#bountysystem, last accessed 22.01.08.
7. See http://www.gnome.org/projects/outreach/a11y/, last accessed 28.06.2008.
8. This was the area of development that the respondents to the survey declared being most active in the six months prior to the survey in July 2005.
9. Bug triaging is a QA process that involves confirming good and reproducible bug reports from the project's bug tracking tools, to establish which actions generate faults in the program. Bug triaging is conducted to resolve invalid and not reproducible bug reports and to prioritize bugs and find and resolve duplicate bug reports.
10. In the case of GNOME, maintainers were identified by text files included in the release tarballs. Because KDE tarballs include very few text files a different strategy was required. A list was compiled of individuals that had 'closed' the most bugs, whom I consider to be 'default' maintainers. Closing bugs involves providing solutions to faults in the program. Maintainers often do this in improving their modules. They frequently submit solutions on behalf of other contributors. All names were cross-referenced with information provided on the module website and confirmed by long-term KDE and GNOME contributors. Maintainers' affiliations were obtained mainly from information provided in the survey because many were members of the

GNOME Foundation and KDE e.V. In some cases affiliation was identified through email aliases and information provided on contributors' blogs and conference schedules.

11. Or departments within companies. It is not possible to assume that large organizations such as IBM and Nokia will have uniform attitudes or understanding of FL/OSS.

12. Learning challenges arising through sponsorship are discussed in West and O'Mahony (2005), who see them as part of the challenge involved in starting up FL/OSS projects initiated by firms.

13. See http://www.linuxformat.co.uk/waugh.html, last accessed 22.06.2008. Shuttleworth's company, Canonical Ltd, developed Ubuntu, one of the most popular Linux distributions based on Debian.

14. Some of these issues are encapsulated by the principal-agent problem in economics which provides a framework for understanding the difficulties employers face in maintaining control over the work of employees under conditions of information asymmetry (Alchian and Demsetz, 1972).

NOTES TO CHAPTER 6

1. They were also questioned on certain aspects of commercialization.

2. This version corresponds to the experimental version of the code that is under development and is different from the stable version that is released for wider use.

3. These 5 developers were also interviewed on certain aspects of commercialization.

4. The role of lurking in the socialization of new developers is highlighted in other studies. Von Krogh, Spaeth and Lakhani (2003) quantify how long developers remain at the periphery, defined by them as a period when emails were posted, but no active contributions were made, and conclude that new contributors post an average of 23 emails before being given the write access to the development tree.

5. Productive in the sense of not merely creating 'noise', see Chapter 5.

6. For details see http://dot.kde.org/1139614608/, last accessed 20.07.2008.

7. The first freeze is usually referred to as the 'feature freeze' and involves finalization of the modules and new features to be included in the release. The second freeze concerns the libraries, the deep-level code that underlies all modules. The third freeze usually relates to the User Interface. The string freeze is the last freeze before the 'hard code freeze', i.e. the final freeze period for translators and documenters to work and the period when minor bugs can be fixed. For more information on the various release phases and freezes of GNOME and KDE, visit http://live.gnome.org/ReleasePlanning/Freezes and http://developer.kde.org/development-versions/release.html, last accessed 04.03.07.

8. At an institutional level, this is reflected in the broadening of the definition of what constitutes a valuable form of contribution which needs to be substantiated in applications for membership to the GNOME Foundation and KDE e.V.

9. See http://lists.kde.org/?l=kde-usability&m=107187409020725&w=2.

10. See http://lists.kde.org/?l=kde-usability&m=107187409020725&w=2.

11. Sun Microsystems Inc. uses GNOME as the default desktop in its Solaris operating system.

12. See http://news.bbc.co.uk/1/hi/business/4602325.stm, last accessed 12.04.2009.

NOTES TO CHAPTER 7

1. As indicated in Chapter 1, the FL/OSS model of development has also been seen as an adaptation and extension of the values and practices of the republic of science (Dasgupta and David, 1994; Polanyi, 1962).
2. This includes Foucault's ideas of relational power and his approach to how to identify and examine power relations, along with work in economic sociology that focuses on the idea of embeddedness and in sociology the CoP perspective.
3. In the context of FL/OSS studies, these findings contribute to the emerging literature that focuses on the role of employees in linking firms and FL/OSS communities (Dahlander and Wallin, 2006; Henkel, 2008; Lin, 2006). They also complement studies concerned with the differentiated roles assumed by contributors within projects that are organized on the basis of a core-periphery scheme (see Chapter 2 for an explanation) by indicating the strong association between employment and core membership (Koch and Schneider, 2002; Long, 2006; Mockus et al., 2002).
4. Theoretically, this aspect of the research clarifies the character of learning relations as relations of power, extending and further developing Lave and Wenger's (1991) initial formulation of the CoP perspective.
5. This aspect contributes to the group of FL/OSS studies that is concerned with the processes of joining and integration of new community members (David and Rullani, 2008; Ducheneaut, 2005; von Krogh et al., 2003).
6. See Chapter 2.
7. In Coleman's (2005) study of the ethical vision behind the Debian community, the issue of meritocracy was also linked to recruitment and the integration of new members.
8. See http://www.gnome.org/press/releases/2008–07-stormy-executive-director .html, last accessed 20.04.2009.
9. For an explanation of this idea, see Chapters 2 and 4.
10. See http://www.linuxworld.com/news/2007/080907-torvalds-on-linux-ms-softwares.html?page=2, last accessed 10.03.2009.
11. Green and Jenkins (2008) develop the idea of the moral economy to examine the commercial appropriation of content and artwork generated by communities of fans. As indicated, they borrow this idea from E. P. Thompson (1971). Connections between morality and economic consumption were also made by Veblen (1927). Silverstone, Hirsch and Morley (1992) discuss the values and experiences that underlie the household as an economic unit of production and consumption in similar terms to those employed in the discussion of the moral economy here.

Bibliography

Alchian, A. A. and Demsetz, H. (1972). 'Production, Information Costs and Economic Organization'. *The American Economic Review* 62(5): 777–95.

Amin, A. and Roberts, J. (eds) (2008). *Community, Economic Creativity and Organization*. Oxford: Oxford University Press.

Anderson, B. (1991). *Imagined Communities: Reflections on the Origin and Spread of Nationalism*. London: Verso.

Arrow, K. (1972). 'Gifts and Exchanges'. *Philosophy and Public Affairs* 1(4): 343–62.

Baldwin, C. Y. and Clark, K. B. (2006). 'The Architecture of Participation: Does Code Architecture Mitigate Free Riding in the Open Source Development Model?' *Management Science* 52(7): 1116–27.

Behlendorf, B. (1999). 'Open Source as a Business Strategy'. In C. DiBona, S. Ockman, and M. Stone (eds) *Open Sources: Voices From the Open Source Revolution*, London: O'Reilly, 149–70.

Benkler, Y. (2002). 'Coase's Penguin, or Linux and the Nature of the Firm'. *Yale Law Journal* 112: 369–446.

——— (2006). *The Wealth of Networks: How Social Production Transforms Markets and Freedom*. New Haven, CT: Yale University Press.

Bertrand, M. and Mullainathan, S. (2001). 'Do People Mean What They Say? Implications for Subjective Survey Data'. *The American Economic Review* 91(2): 67–72.

Bird, C., Gourley, A., Devanbu, P., Gertz, M. and Swaminathan, A. (2006). 'Mining Email Social Networks'. In S. Diehl, H. Gall and A. E. Hassan (eds) *Proceedings of 3rd International Workshop on Mining Software Repositories, 22–23 May, Shanghai, China,* New York: ACM, 137–43.

Bonaccorsi, A. and Rossi, C. (2006). 'Comparing Motivations of Individual Programmers and Firms to Take Part in the Open Source Movement: From Community to Business'. *Knowledge, Technology & Policy* 18(4): 40–64.

Brabham, D. C. (2008). 'Crowdsourcing as a Model for Problem Solving'. *Convergence: The International Journal of Research into New Media Technologies* 14(1): 75–90.

Braudel, F. (1982). *Civilization & Capitalism 15th–18th Century: Perspectives of the World*. (Vol. 3), London: Phoenix Press.

Brooks, F. (1995). *The Mythical Man-Month: Essays on Software Engineering* (20th Anniversary Ed.). Reading, MA: Addison-Wesley.

Brown, J. S. and Duguid, P. (2000). *The Social Life of Information*. Boston, MA: Harvard Business School Press.

——— (2001). 'Knowledge and Organization: A Social-Practice Perspective'. *Organization Science* 12(2): 198–213.

Capiluppi, A. and Milchmayr, M. (2007). 'From the Cathedral to the Bazaar: An Empirical Study of the Lifecycle of Volunteer Community Projects'. In J. Feller, B. Fitzgerald, W. Scacchi and A. Sillitti (eds) *Open Source Development, Adoption and Innovation: Proceedings of IFIP Working Group 2.13 on Open Source Software, 11–14 June, Limerick, Ireland*, Boston, MA: Springer Boston, 31–44.

Castells, M. (2001). *The Internet Galaxy*. Oxford and New York: Oxford University Press.

Cheal, D. (1988). *The Gift Economy*. London: Routledge.

Chesbrough, H. W. (2006). *Open Innovation: The New Imperative From Creating and Profiting From Technology*. Boston, MA: Harvard Business School Press.

Coase, R. (1937). 'The Nature of the Firm'. *Economica* 4(16): 386–405.

Coleman, G. (2004). 'The Political Agnosticism of Free and Open Source Software and the Inadvertent Politics of Contrast'. *Anthropological Quarterly* 77(3): 507–19.

——— (2005). 'Three Ethical Moments in Debian: The Making of the Ethical Hacker'. Ch. 6 in Doctoral Dissertation 'The Social Construction of Freedom in Free and Open Source Software: Hackers, Ethics and the Liberal Tradition', Department of Anthropology, University of Chicago, Ill.

Conklin, M. (2006). 'Beyond Low Hanging Fruit: Seeking the Next Generation in Floss Data Mining'. In E. Damiani, B. Fitzgerald, W. Scacchi and M. Scotto (eds) *Open Source Systems: Proceedings of IFIP Working Group 2.13 on Open Source Software, 8–10 June, Como, Italy,* Boston, MA: Springer Boston, 47–56.

Cross, R. and Parker A. (2004). *The Hidden Power of Social Networks: Understanding How Work Really Gets Done in Organizations*. Boston, MA: Harvard Business School Press.

Crowston, K. and Howison, J. (2005). 'The Social Structure of Free and Open Source Software Development'. *First Monday:* 10(2), http://firstmonday.org/htbin/cgi-wrap/bin/ojs/index.php/fm/article/view/1207/1127, accessed 10.05.2009.

Dahlander, L., Frederiksen, L. and Rullani, F. (2008). 'Online Communities and Open Innovation: Governance and Symbolic Value Creation'. *Industry and Innovation* 15(2): 115–23.

Dahlander, L. and Wallin, M. W. (2006). 'A Man on the Inside: Unlocking Communities as Complementary Assets'. *Research Policy* 35(8): 1243–59.

Dasgupta, P. and David, P. A. (1994). 'Towards a New Economics of Science'. *Research Policy* 23(5): 487–521.

David, P. A. and Rullani, F. (2008). 'Dynamics of Innovation in an "Open Source" Collaboration Environment: Lurking, Laboring and Launching Floss Projects on Sourceforge'. *Industrial and Corporate Change* 17(4): 647–710.

David, P. A. and Shapiro, J. (2008). 'Community Based Production: What Do We Know About the Developers Who Participate?' *Information Economics and Policy* 20(4): 364–98.

David, P.A., Waterman, A. and Arora, S. (2003). *FLOSS-US the Free/Libre/Open Source Developer Software Survey for 2003: A First Report*. Stanford, CA: SIEPR—Stanford Institute for Economic and Policy Research, http://www.stanford.edu/group/floss-us/report/FLOSS-US-Report.pdf, accessed 10.05.2009.

Demil, B. and Lecocq, X. (2006). 'Neither Market, Nor Hierarchy Or Network: The Emerging Bazaar Governance'. *Organization Studies* 27(10): 1447–66.

Ducheneaut, N. (2005). 'Socialization in an Open Source Software Community: A Socio-Technical Analysis'. *Computer Supported Cooperative Work* 14(4): 323–68.

Duguid, P. (2003). 'Incentivizing Practice'. In Y. P. René van Bavel, J.-C. Burgelman, I. Tuomi and B. Clements (eds) *ICTs and Social Capital in the Information Society: Report on a Joint DG JRC/DG Employment Workshop,* Seville: Institute for Prospective Technological Studies/European Commission, 83–116.

Fitzgerald, B. (2006). 'The Transformation of Open Source Software'. *MIS Quarterly* 30(3): 587–98.

Fosfuri, A., Girratana, M. S. and Luzzi, A. (2008). 'The Penguin has Entered the Building: The Commercialization of Open Source Software Projects'. *Organization Science* 19(2): 292–305.

Foucault, M. (1979). *Discipline and Punish: The Birth of the Prison*. Harmondsworth: Penguin.

—— (1981). 'The Order of Discourse'. In R. Young (ed.) *Untying the Text: A Post-Structuralist Reader*. Boston and London: Routledge and Kegan Paul, 48–78.

—— (1982a). 'The Subject and Power'. In by J. D. Faubion (ed.) *Michel Foucault: Power/Essential Works of Foucault 1954–1984. Vol. 3*, London and New York: Penguin Books, 326–48.

—— (1982b). 'The Political Technology of Individuals'. In J. D. Faubion (ed.) *Michel Foucault: Power/Essential Works of Foucault 1954–1984. Vol. 3*, London and New York: Penguin Books, 403–17.

—— (1982c). 'Technologies of the Self'. In J. D. Faubion (ed.) *Michel Foucault: Ethics/Essential Works of Foucault 1954–1984. Vol.1*, London and New York: Penguin Books, 223–51.

—— (2002). 'Questions of Method'. In J. D. Faubion (ed.) *Michel Foucault: Power/Essential Works of Foucault 1954–1984. Vol. 3*, New York: New Press, 223–38.

Frey, B. S. and Jegen, F. (2001). 'Motivation Crowding Theory'. *Journal of Economic Surveys* 15(5): 589–611.

Friedman, N. and Icaza, M. (2005). 'Mechanics of Open Source: Growing and Harvesting Your Project'. Presentation to The Massachussets Software Council, June, available at: http://www.nat.org/2005/june/MassSoftware.pdf, accessed 22.09.2008.

Gasser, L., Ripoche, G. and Sandusky, R. J. (2004). 'Research Infrastucture for Empirical Science of F/OSS'. In A. Hassan, R. C. Holt and A. Mockus (eds) *ICSE Workshop on Mining Software Repositories, 25 May, Edinburgh, Scotland,* New York: IEEE Computer Society, 80–4.

Ghosh, R. A. (2005). 'Understanding Free Software Developers: Findings From the Floss Study'. In J. Feller, B. Fitzgerald, S. A. Hissam and K. R. Lakhani (eds) *Perspectives on Free and Open Source Software*, Cambridge, MA: The MIT Press, 23–46.

Ghosh, R. A., Glott, R., Krieger, B. and Robles, G. (2002). *Free/Libre and Open Source Software Survey and Study: Part 4, Survey of Developers,* Maastricht: University of Maastricht, available at: http://www.infonomics.nl/FLOSS/report/FLOSS_Final4.pdf, accessed 22.02.2009.

Ghosh, R. A. (2006). 'Study on the Economic Impact of Open Source Software on the Innovation and Competitiveness of the Information and Communication Technologies Sector in the EU'. Report prepared for the European Commission, contract no. ENTR/04/112, available at http://ec.europa.eu/enterprise/ict/policy/doc/2006–11–20-flossimpact.pdf, accessed 02.05.2008.

Ghosh, R. A. (2002). 'Clustering and Dependencies in Free/Open Source Development: A Methodology'. Paper presented at IDEI/CEPR Workshop on 'Open Source Software: Economics, Law and Policy', 20–21 June, Toulouse, France, available at: http://dxm.org/papers/toulouse2/cluster-final.pdf, accessed 23.09.2008.

Ghosh, R. A. and David, P. A. (2003). 'The Nature and Composition of the Linux Kernel Developer Community: A Dynamic Analysis'. *SIEPR-Project NOSTRA Working Paper*, draft version 5, available at: http://dxm.org/papers/licks1/licksresults.pdf, accessed 02.06.2009.

Goffman, E. (1969). *Where The Action Is—Three Essays*. London: Allen Lane-The Penguin Press, 4–36.

Goldman, R. and Gabriel, R. P. (2005). *Innovation Happens Elsewhere: Open Source as a Business Strategy*. San Francisco, CA: Morgan Kaufmann.

González-Barahona, J. M., Martínez, A., Reyes, M., Hierro, J. J., Javier, S. and Fernández, R. (2008). 'The Networked Forge: New Environments for Libre Software Development'. In B. Russo, E. Damiani, S. Hissam, B. Lundell, and G. Succi (eds) *Open Source Development, Communities and Quality: Proceedings of IFIP Working Group 2.13 on Open Source Software, 7–10 September, Milan, Italy*, Boston, MA: Springer Boston, 299–306.

Granovetter, M. (1985). 'Economic Action and Social Structure: The Problem of Embeddedness'. *The American Journal of Sociology* 91(3): 481–510.

Green, J. and Jenkins, H. (2008). 'The Moral Economy of Web 2.0: Audience Research and Convergence Culture'. Parts of a White Paper included in blog confessions of an Aca-Fan, available at: http://henryjenkins.org/2008/03/the_moral_economy_of_web_20_pa.html, accessed 10.01.2009.

Haas, P. M. (1992). 'Introduction: Epistemic Communities and International Policy Coordination'. *International Organization* 46(1): 1–35.

Haruvy, E., Prasad, A. and Sethi, S. P. (2003). 'Harvesting Altruism in Open-Source Software Development'. *Journal of Optimization Theory and Applications* 118(2): 381–416.

Henkel, J. (2008). 'Champions of Revealing: The Role of Open Source Developers in Commercial Firms'. Draft available at: http://papers.ssrn.com/sol3/papers.cfm?abstract_id=946929, accessed 22.02.2008.

Hertel, G., Niedner, S. and Herrmann, S. (2003). 'Motivation of Software Developers in Open Source Projects: An Internet-Based Survey of Contributors to the Linux Kernel'. *Research Policy* 32(7): 1159–77.

Hicks, D. (1995). 'Published Papers, Tacit Competencies and Corporate Management of the Public/Private Character of Knowledge'. *Industrial and Corporate Change* 4(2): 401–24.

Hill, M. B. (2002). 'The Geeks Shall Inherit the Earth: My History of Unlearning'. Paper available at: http://mako.cc/writing/unlearningstory/StoryOfUnlearing.pdf, accessed 22.02.2008.

Himanen, P. (2001). *The Hacker Ethic and the Spirit of the Information Age*. London: Vintage.

Howison, J., Conklin, M. and Crowston, K. (2006). 'Flossmole: A Collaborative Repository for Floss Research Data and Analysis'. *International Journal of Information Technology and Web Engineering* 1(3): 17–26.

Jaaksi, A. (2007). 'Experiences on Product Development with Open Source Software'. In J. Feller, B. Fitzerald, W. Scacchi, and A. Sillitti (eds) *Open Source Development, Adoption and Innovation: Proceedings of IFIP Working Group 2.13 on Open Source Software, 11–14 June, Limerick, Ireland*, Boston, MA: Springer Boston, 85–96.

Jenkins, H., Xiaochang, L., Domb Krauskopf, A. and Green, J. (2009). 'If It Doesn't Spread, It's Dead'. White Paper, presented serialized form on the blog 'Confessions of an Aca-Fan', available at: http://henryjenkins.org/2009/02/if_it_doesnt_spread_its_dead_p.html, accessed 09.03.2009.

Kidder, T. (2000). *The Soul of a New Machine*. Boston, MA: Back Bay Books.

Kittur, A., B. Pendleton, and Mytkowicz, T. (2007). 'Power of the Few Vs. Wisdom of the Crowd: Wikipedia and the Rise of the Bourgeoise'. Paper presented at 25th Annual ACM Conference on Human Factors in Computing Systems, San Jose, CA.

Knorr-Cetina, K. (1999). *Epistemic Cultures*. Cambridge, MA: Harvard University Press.

Koch, S. and Schneider, G. (2002). 'Effort, Co-Ordination and Co-Operation in an Open Source Software Project: GNOME'. *Information Systems Journal* 12(1): 27–42.

Krishnamurthy, S. (2002). 'Cave or Community? An Empirical Examination of 100 Mature Open Source Projects'. *First Monday,* 6(7), http://www.firstmonday.dk/issues/issue7_6/krishnamurthy/index.html, accessed 05.05.2004.
—— (2005). 'An Analysis of Open Source Business Models'. In J. Feller, B. Fitzgerald, S. A. Hissam, and K. R. Lakhani (eds) *Perspectives on Free and Open Source Software,* Cambridge, MA: The MIT Press, 279–96.
—— (2006). 'On the Intrinsic and Extrinsic Motivations of Free/Libre/Open Source (Floss) Developers'. *Knowledge, Technology & Policy* 18(4): 17–39.
Kroah-Hartman, G., Corbet, J. and, McPherson, A. (2008). 'From the Linux Foundation: How Fast It Is Going, Who Is Doing It, What They Are Doing, and Who Is Sponsoring It'. Online Report available at: http://www.linux-foundation.org/publications/linuxkerneldevelopment.php, accessed 05.05.2008.
Lakhani, K. (2006). 'The Core and Periphery in Distributed and Self-Organizing Systems'. Doctoral Dissertation, Sloan School of Management, MIT.
Lakhani, K. R. and Wolf, R. G. (2005). 'Why Hackers Do What They Do: Understanding Motivation and Effort in Free/Open Source Software Projects'. In J. Feller, B. Fitzgerald, S. A. Hissam and K. R. Lakhani (eds) *Perspectives on Free and Open Source Software,* Cambridge, MA: The MIT Press, 3–22.
Lave, J. and Wenger, E. (1991). *Situated Learning: Legitimate Peripheral Participation.* Cambridge: Cambridge University Press.
Lazer, D., Pentland, A., Adamic, L., Aral, S., Barabási, A.-L., Brewer, D., Christakis, N., Contractor, N., Fowler, J., Gutmann, M., Jebara, T., King, G., Macy, M., Roy, D. and Van Alstyne, M. (2009). 'Computational Social Science'. *Science* 323(5915): 721–23.
Lerner, J. and Tirole, J. (2002). 'Some Simple Economics of Open Source'. *Journal of Industrial Economics* 50(2): 197–234.
—— (2005). 'The Scope of Open Source Licensing'. *Journal of Law, Economics and Organization* 21(1): 20–56.
Lessig, L. (2002). 'Open Source Baselines: Compared to What?' In R. W. Hahn (ed.) *Government Policy Toward Open Source Software,* Washington DC: AEI-Brookings Joint Centre For Regulatory Studies.
—— (2008). *Remix-Making Art and Commerce Thrive in the Hybrid Economy.* New York: Penguin Press.
Levy, S. (1984). *Hackers: Heroes of the Computer Revolution.* Garden City, NY: Doubleday.
Lin, Y. (2006). 'Hybrid Innovation: The Dynamics of Collaboration Between the Floss Community and Corporations'. *Knowledge, Technology & Policy* 18(4): 86–100.
Linus, T. and Diamond, D. (2001). *Just for Fun: The Story of an Accidental Revolutionary.* New York: Harper Business.
Long, J. (2006). 'Understanding the Role of Core Developers in Open Source Software Development'. *Journal of Information, Information Technology and Organizations* 1: 75–85.
Love, R. (2005). *Linux Kernel Development, Second Edition.* Indianapolis: Novell Press.
Mateos-Garcia, J. and Steinmueller, W. E. (2008). 'The Institutions of Open Source Software: Examining the Debian Community'. *Information, Economics and Policy* 20(4): 333–44.
Michlmayr, M. (2007). 'Quality Improvement in Volunteer Free and Open Source Software Projects'. Doctoral Dissertation, Centre for Technology Management, Institute for Manufacturing, University of Cambridge.
Mockus, A., Fielding, R. T. and Herbsleb (2002). 'Two Case Studies of Open Source Software Development: Apache and Mozilla'. *ACM Transactions on Software Engineering and Methodology* 11(3): 309–46.

Moody, G. (2001). *Rebel Code: Inside Linux and the Open Source Revolution.* New York: Perseus Press.

Mustonen, M. (2005). 'When Does a Firm Substitute Open Source Programming?' *Journal of Economics and Management Strategy* 14(1): 121–39.

North, D. C. (2008). 'Institutions and Credible Commitment'. *SSN Working Paper* available at: http://papers.ssrn.com/sol3/Papers.cfm?abstract_id=6042, accessed 22.02.2009.

O'Mahony, C. S. (2002). 'The Emergence of a New Commercial Actor: Community Managed Software Projects'. Doctoral Dissertation, Department of Management Science and Engineering Management. Stanford University.

—— (2007). 'The Governance of Open Source Initiatives: What Does it Mean to be Community Managed?' *Journal of Management and Governance* 11: 139–50.

O'Mahony, C. S. and J. West (2005). 'What Makes a Project Open Source? Migrating from Organic to Synthetic Communities'. Paper presented at Academy of Management Conference, Technology and Innovation Management Division, Honolulu.

O'Reilly, T. (2005). 'The Open Source Paradigm Shift'. In J. Feller, B. Fitzgerald, S. A. Hissam and K. R. Lakhani (eds) *Perspectives on Free and Open Source Software*, Cambridge, MA: MIT Press, 461–82.

Polanyi, K. (1944). *The Great Transformation: The Political and Economic Origins of Our Time.* Boston: Beacon Press.

—— (1962). 'The Republic of Science: Its Political and Economic Theory'. *Minerva* 1(1): 54–73.

Rainer, A. and S. Gale (2005). 'Evaluating the Quality and Quantity of Data on Open Source Software Projects'. M. Scotto and G. Succi (eds) *Proceedings of the First International Conference on Open Source Systems, Genova, 11th–15th July*, pp. 29–36, available at: http://oss2005.case.unibz.it/Papers/14.pdf, accessed 22.03.2009.

Raymond, E. S. (2001). *The Cathedral and the Bazaar: Musings on Linux and Open Source by an Accidental Revolutionary.* Sebastopol, CA: O'Reilly.

Roberts, J., Hann, I.-H. and Slaughter, S. (2006). 'Understanding the Motivations, Participation, and Performance of Open Source Software Developers: A Longitudinal Study of the Apache Projects'. *Management Science* 52(7): 984–99.

Robles, G. (2005). 'Empirical Software Engineering Research on Libre Software: Data Sources, Methodologies and Results'. Doctoral Dissertation, Department of Informatics, Statistics and Telematics, Universidad Rey Juan Carlos.

Robles, G., Duenas, S. and González-Barahona, J. M. (2007). 'Corporate Involvement in Libre Sofware: Study of the Presence in Debian Code Over Time'. In J. Feller, B. Fitzerald, W. Scacchi and A. Sillitti (eds) *Open Source Development, Adoption and Innovation*, Boston, MA: Springer Boston, 121–32.

Rose, N. (1999). *Powers of Freedom: Reframing Political Thought.* Cambridge: Cambridge University Press.

Rosenberg, N. (1989). 'Why Do Firms Do Basic Research (With Their Own Money?)'. *Research Policy* 19(2): 165–74.

Rosenkopf, L. and Tushman, M. (1994). 'The Coevolution of Community Networks and Technology: Lessons From the Flight Simulation Industry'. *Industrial and Corporate Change* 7(2): 311–14.

Schaefer, R. (2006). 'A Critical Programmer Searches for Professionalism'. *ACM SIGSOFT Software Engineering Notes* 31(4): 1–17.

Shah, S. K. (2006). 'Motivation, Governance, and the Viability of Hybrid Forms in Open Source Software Development'. *Management Science* 52(7): 1000–14.

Shepsle, K. A. (1991). 'Discretion Institutions and the Problem of Government'. In P. Bourdieu and J. S. Coleman (eds) *Social Theory for a Changing Society*, Boulder, CO: Western Press, 245–62.

Shirky, C. (2005). 'Institutions Vs. Collaboration'. Presentation at the TEDGlobal Conference, July, Oxford, available at: http://www.ted.com/talks/clay_shirky_on_institutions_versus_collaboration.html, accessed 03.05.2009.

Silverstone, R., Hirsch, E. and Morley, D. (1992). 'Information and Communication Technologies and the Moral Economy of the Household'. In R. Silverstone, and E. Hirsch (eds) *Consuming Technologies: Media and Information in Domestic Spaces*, London: Routledge, 15–31.

Steinmueller, W. E. (2003). 'Communities of Practice and Their Effects on Performance and Functioning of Organizations'. In Y. P. René van Bavel, J.-C. Burgelman, I. Tuomi and B. Clements (eds) *ICTs and Social Capital in the Knowledge Society-Report on a JRC/DG Employment Workshop*, Seville: Institute for Prospective Technological Studies–IPTS, 51–75.

Stewart, K. J., Ammeter, A. P. and Maruping, L. M. (2005). 'A Preliminary Analysis of Influences of Licensing and Organizational Sponsorship on Success in Open Source Projects'. *HICCS' 05 Proceedings of the 38th Hawaii International Conference on System Sciences, 3–6 January, Big Island, Hawaii*, IEEE Computer Society, available at: http://doi.ieeecomputersociety.org/10.1109/HICSS.2005.38, accessed 20.11.2009.

Strahilevitz, L. J. (2007). 'Wealth Without Markets?' *Yale Law Journal* 116(70): 1472–1517.

Studer, M. (2007). 'Community Structure, Individual Participation and the Social Construction of Merit'. In J. Feller, B. Fitzgerald, W. Scacchi and A. Sillitti (eds) *Open Source Development, Adoption and Innovation: Proceedings of IFIP Working Group 2.13 on Open Source Software, 11–14 June, Limerick*, Boston, MA: Springer Boston, 161–72.

Swan, J., Scarbrough, H. and Robertson, M. (2002). 'The Construction of "Communities of Practice" in the Management of Innovation'. *Management Learning* 33(4): 477–96.

Tanur, J. M. (1992). *Questions About Questions: Inquiries Into the Cognitive Bases of Surveys*. New York: Russell Sage.

Teece, D. J. (1986). 'Profiting from Technological Innovation: Implications for Integration, Collaboration, Licensing and Public Policy'. *Research Policy* 15(6): 285–305.

Thompson, E. P. (1971). 'The Moral Economy of the English Crowd in the Eighteenth Century'. *Past and Present* 50(1): 76–136.

Thrift, N. (2006). 'Re-Inventing Invention: New Tendencies in Capitalist Commodification'. *Economy and Society* 35(2): 279–306.

Titmuss, R. (1971). *The Gift Relationship: From Human Blood to Social Policy*. London: George Allen and Unwin.

Tuomi, I. (2004). 'Evolution of the Linux Credit File: Methodological Challenges and Reference Data for Open Source Research'. *First Monday*, 9(6): available at: http://www.firstmonday.org/ISSUES/issue9_6/tuomi/index.html, accessed 22.02.2008.

Veblen, T. (1921). *The Engineers and the Price System*. New York: Cossimo Classics.
—— (1927). *The Theory of the Leisure Class: An Economic Study of Institutions*. New York: Vanguard Press.

von Hippel, E. (2007). 'Horizontal Innovation Networks—By and for Users'. *Industrial and Corporate Change* 16(2): 293–315.

von Hippel, E. and von Krogh, G. (2003). 'Open Source Software and the "Private-Collective" Innovation Model: Issues for Organization Science'. *Organization Science* 14(2): 209–23.

von Krogh, G. and Spaeth, S. (2007). 'The Open Source Software Phenomenon: Characteristics that Promote Research'. *Journal of Strategic Information Systems* 16: 236–53.

von Krogh, G., Spaeth, S. and Lakhani, K. R. (2003). 'Community, Joining and Specialization in Open Source Software Innovation: A Case Study'. *Research Policy* 32(7): 1217–41.

Wenger, E. (1998). *Communities of Practice: Learning, Meaning and Identity.* Cambridge: Cambridge University Press.

Wenger, E., McDermot, R. and Snyder, W. M. (2002). *Cultivating Communities of Practice: A Guide to Managing Knowledge.* Boston, MA: Harvard Business School Press.

West, J. (2003). 'How Open is Open Enough? Melding Proprietary and Open Source Platform Strategies'. *Research Policy* 32(7): 1259–85.

—— (2007). 'Value Capture and Value Networks in Open Source Vendors Strategies'. *HICCS' 07* Proceedings of the *40th Hawaii International Conference on System Sciences, 3–6 January, Big Island, Hawaii,* IEEE Computer Society: available at: http://doi.ieeecomputersociety.org/10.1109/HICSS.2007.600, accessed 20.11.2009.

West, J. and Gallagher, S. (2006). 'Challenges of Open Innovation: The Paradox of Firm Investment in Open Source Software'. *R&D Management* 36(3): 319–31.

West, J. and O'Mahony, C. S. (2005). 'Contrasting Community Building in Sponsored and Community Founded Open Source Projects'. *HICCS' 05 Proceedings of the 38th Hawaii International Conference on System Sciences,* IEEE Computer Society: available at: http://doi.ieeecomputersociety.org/10.1109/HICSS.2005.166, accessed 20.11.2009.

—— (2008). 'The Role of Participation Architecture in Growing Sponsored Open Source Communities'. *Industry and Innovation* 15(3): 145–68.

Williamson, E. O. (1987). *The Economic Institutions of Capitalism: Firms, Market, Relational Contracting.* London: The Free Press.

Yu, L. and Ramaswamy, S. (2007). 'Mining CVS Repositories to Understand Open-Source Project Developer Roles'. *Proceedings of the 4th International Workshop on Mining Software Repositories, 19–20 May, Minneapolis,* Washington DC: IEEE Computer Society.

Yu, L., S. Ramaswamy and M. Zhang (2008). 'Mining Email Archives and Simulating the Dynamics of Open-Source Project Developer Networks', *Proceedings of the 4th International Workshop on Enterprise and Organizational Modelling and Simulation, 16–17 June Montpellier, France,* Atlanta: AIS, 17–31.

Zuboff, S. (1988). *In the Age of the Smart Machine: The Future of Work and Power.* New York: Basic Books.

Index